SOFTBALL'S LEFTY LEGEND

SOFTBALL'S LEFTY LEGEND
TY STOFFLET

By
Steven Clarfield, Ph.D.

With Special Contribution by
Bill Plummer III

Foreword by
Ron Radigonda

Introduction by
Bill Howell

Clear Vision Publishing, Inc.
2004

Published by Clear Vision Publishing, Inc.
301 Highway 9 South,
Manalapan, New Jersey   07726

Copyright © 2004 by Steven Clarfield, Ph.D.

All rights reserved. No part of this book may be used or reproduced in any manner whatsoever, electronic, mechanical, photocopying, recording or otherwise, without the prior written permission of the publisher.

ISBN 0-9758541-0-0

Produced by www.booksprintedhere.com
Manahawkin Printing
Printed in Canada
****

To Kathy Stofflet, Patricia Clarfield
&
All the Spouses Who Encourage
Players to Enjoy the Game.

Preface

IN THE 25-YEAR PERIOD between 1967 and 1992, Ty Stofflet established a set of records in national and world softball tournaments sanctioned by either the International Softball Congress (ISC), the Amateur Softball Association of America (ASA) or the International Softball Federation (ISF) that puts him in the category of one of the all-time greats of the game.

His career was sufficiently illustrious and lengthy to enable him to set standards for both the ISC and the ASA even though for most of his career he was able to play in only one sanctioning body's events within a calendar year. ISC events belong to the decade of the '60s, while the ASA years are comprised of the '70s and '80s. From 1984 on, he was able to compete in both ISC and ASA events, which he did until completing his championship participation in 1992 at age 51.

In three separate years, he was voted Most Valuable Player in the ISC World Tournament – 1967, 1968, 1969. He was the ASA selection for Most Valuable Player in 1971, 1974, 1975, 1977 and 1978.

In his only ISF tournament (1976), playing for the USA in New Zealand, he was voted both Most Valuable Player and Most Valuable Pitcher. But the records don't begin to tell the story of the man who became the standard by which all players of his generation are judged.

Foreword
by Ron Radigonda

IT IS A PLEASURE FOR ME to write this introduction for one of the truly great softball pitchers of all-time, Ty Stofflet.

Although I played fast pitch earlier in my career, I never got a chance to see Ty pitch. I wish I had. I can assure you, however, that his exploits and achievements were well known on the West Coast.

It is fitting and appropriate for a book to be written about Ty's career. Ty learned the value of hard work as a teenager and, with the help of his dad, Harold, honed and refined his skills to become one of the game's best in a career that spanned 40 years.

Ty's accomplishments, as you would imagine, generated considerable media coverage and helped boost the ASA's Men's Major Fast Pitch program. Ty not only was a sportsman on the field but off the field as well. Although now retired as an active player, he still finds time to tutor aspiring pitchers in his hometown of Coplay, PA.

In November, Ty will be inducted into the ASA National Softball Hall of Fame during our National Council Meeting in Mobile, AL. It is for a career that will be difficult to equal, let alone surpass.

Ty indeed was "Softball's Lefty Legend" and his induction into the ASA National Hall of Fame is a fitting recognition for an athlete who time and again thrilled fans from the eight-foot circle.

Introduction
by Bill Howell

UNTIL THE EARLY 1980s, the Amateur Softball Association (ASA), which is the national governing body of softball in the United States, prohibited its sanctioned teams from participating in ISC competition. Through the 1950s and early 60s, the International Softball Congress (ISC) was comprised of teams mostly from the Midwest to California. There were very few, if any, teams from the East Coast to participate in its competition.

In 1963, the Allentown Patriots won an ISC qualifying tournament and accepted a bid to participate in the ISC's championship tournament. The Patriots were led by a 22-year-old-phenom from Coplay, PA, Ty Stofflet, who threw hard but hadn't as yet learned the intricacies of pitching. Nevertheless, some people within the ISC recognized the star power that Stofflet projected because he was voted the most popular player in the ISC Tournament two years in a row. In a few short years that star power was evident for all to see because in 1967 and again in 1969 Ty was selected as the MVP of the ISC World Tournament. In 1969, his team, Sal's Lunch, scored a total of seven runs over five tournament games, yet won the ISC World Tournament because Ty Stofflet didn't allow the opposition to score while striking out 86 in 42 innings.

At 28, Stofflet was just coming into the prime of his fast pitch career. But, because of the ASA restrictions, Ty would not pitch another game in the ISC until 1984 when

Softball's Lefty Legend ~ Ty Stofflet

he was 43 years-old. When he returned he picked up right where he left off and was selected to the ISC All-World Team. Even more amazing is that in 1992, at age 51, Ty won four games in the ISC World Tournament and was once again selected to the ISC All-World Team. Ty is sixth on the all-time list for wins in the ISC World Tournament with 38. It's hard to imagine what that number could have been.

On a more personal note, I've known Ty for more than 30 years. My perspective on him comes from the opposing dugout (for many years) as a manager in his later fast pitch career and as a catcher and teammate for several years in the "Over 40" division of play. Ty is one of the best ambassadors ever for men's fast pitch softball. Having been with him in cities across the United States, I have seen fans approach him and introduce themselves. Often these people would have their son or daughter with them. They would say they had seen Ty pitch in such and such a tournament in such and such a year and would strike up a conversation with him. He had a natural way of making that brief exchange a very enjoyable experience. Most of the time they would request that he sign a ball or some other article for them. Ty never missed a beat with these people. He treated them as if they were old friends, although he didn't know many of them prior to that conversation. Ty would shake their hands, sign their items and talk to them with a smile. They would walk away talking with their children and in some cases their grandchildren, and all left with a greater appreciation of the game and the man.

When it comes to talking about all-time greats, it is always a very subjective discussion. If in some mythical world I had to choose one pitcher at the height of his career to win one game, I wouldn't hesitate. Ty Stofflet would be my pitcher.

Table of Contents

Preface vii
Foreword ix
Introduction xi
Prologue xv

Profile of a Softball Legend ~ The Early Years

"The Ferocious Gentleman"....................... 3

The Sunners ~ The Quest to be the Best

Making Connections............................... 35
The Weekend from Hell........................... 39
A New Year ~ A Renewed Set of Hopes .. 47
Ty's Growing Fan Base 65
Starting All Over Again........................... 69
The Team Refuses to Stand Still................ 75
When Life Presents Obstacles................... 81
Bringing it Home.................................... 87
America's Team....................................... 99
A Fast Pitch Game for the Ages
   by Bill Plummer III.................................. 103
After the Ball is Over............................... 115
The Gang's All Here ~ Let's Have a Party
Hail the Conquering Heroes..................... 123
How Do You Spell Dynasty? 137

Softball's Lefty Legend ~ Ty Stofflet

Coping with Change

What a Difference a Moment Makes............	163
The Return of the Tiger	167
Getting Back to Championship Form?.........	172
Taking a Run at Two Titles..........................	181
Gaining Perspective	196
Wrapping It Up..	203
Finishing Up Strong.....................................	209

Epilogue

Ty Stofflet in the Lehigh Valley.....................	221
Acknowledgements..	229
Photo Credits..	232

Prologue

THIS BOOK MUST contain a caveat. Throughout these pages, a number of people, including some 20 softball experts, recall stories regarding the era in which Ty Stofflet was fast pitch softball's dominant player. He was also, arguably, one of its finest ambassadors.

For anyone who knows Ty, it will be clear that he has very little use for self-aggrandizement. Therefore, those of us who have made statements that pertain to Ty in this book are clearly expressing our personal points of view. His response to questions about himself? "It makes no sense to talk about yourself. Do the deeds and let others provide the stories."

Softball players are inveterate storytellers. Get any of them together and we start offering comparisons. "Who was the best hitter you ever faced? Who was the best pitcher?," etc. In the same way that the nasty old witch in Sleeping Beauty kept asking her "mirror, mirror on the wall" for information, players, coaches and interested fans of the game have carried on a running conversation regarding "Who is best?," most likely for as long as there has been a game.

Having lived in New Jersey and having played during the '70s, I can remember asking a tough old pitcher named Sammy Ardolino who he thought was the best pitcher in

Softball's Lefty Legend ~ Ty Stofflet

our area. Sammy was one of those guys who could throw two games a night for two different teams and sometimes three if he had to. And he could do it four nights a week. Sammy's face broke out into a big smile, as he readied his answer.

"I've seen them all, and there is only one Ty," he said. "He is just that much better than everybody else." With that he set an imaginary line with his right pitching arm. "Everybody else is here," said Sam, holding his arm out at about chest height. "Ty is here," he finished, moving his hand to eye level. Enough said.

Sammy's certainty was something that stuck with me. I had never heard anyone talk about "the best" with such certainty.

At various league games, I would pick up tidbits about Ty. He was reported to be consistently very generous with any pitcher who asked him for help. He couldn't give them 10 to 20 miles more per hour on their fastball, but he could help them work on his favorite pitch, the changeup.

One summer night in 1978, the Poughkeepsie Brewers were playing the Reading team that Ty pitched for. They were a tough hitting "AA" team that played in the Seaboard League against the best competition around. Surely they would provide a good test.

My dad, Bob Clarfield, and I watched Ty on the sidelines with his catcher, soft tossing at double pitching distance. He seemed smaller than Sammy's description led me to believe, but that may have been because my experience of top fast pitch pitchers conjured up visions of guys about 6'2" who weighed in at 240 pounds.

The game was truly a revelation. Rather than maintaining his relaxed manner, he was coiled and dangerous. Each pitch appeared to be shot from a cannon in a flurry of dust. From my position in the middle of the stands, I watched a

Prologue

pitcher display the ability to focus fully and release completely. The ball wasn't so much pitched as it was made to explode. And the guy could do it pitch after pitch after pitch.

Ty went through the Poughkeepsie lineup like they weren't even there. Hitters that I had seen tear the cover off the ball were overmatched. And what was more to the point, they knew it. There was no anger when they struck out, just a brief walk back to the bench and a return of the bat to the bat rack.

The Reading team, while attentive, had very little to do while Ty was pitching. Just a popup here, or a grounder there. Nothing hit very hard. There were lots of strikeouts and maybe a couple of hits. Visions of the famed Eddie Feigner's traveling troubadours (The King and His Court) danced in my head, but the Brewers had the potential to be lethal, whereas Feigner had moved much more toward pure entertainment. I also thought of the years when Satchel Paige told his teammates to sit down while he struck out the other side, but that again had flamboyance that didn't match this scene.

Ty Stofflet was just being Ty Stofflet. If the other team had the nerve to step on the same softball diamond with him, well, they were going to get a full dose of the man they were facing. I nearly felt sorry for the other team, except that they didn't seem to mind. Today was their day to face the best. Maybe he would make the next guy they faced look a lot easier to hit.

The game moved along for 10 innings until the Reading team scored a run. In the bottom of the inning, the leadoff batter, Ronnie Kist from New Jersey, bunted and, after a misplay into the outfield, went all the way to third. The classic softball or baseball situation is about to

Softball's Lefty Legend ~ Ty Stofflet

unfold: fast runner on third, no outs, and the 2, 3 and 4 batters coming to the plate. Now we get to see how this pitcher who has had his way throughout the game deals with the error that has put him in this pickle.

The No. 2 hitter goes down on three rise balls. Strike one, strike two, strike three. Everything related to Ty is moving now at slightly greater speed. The arms are going up behind the head a little faster. The arms are going behind the body a little faster, and the windmill circle is just a bit more of a blur. One thing remains the same, however. Wherever the catcher's glove is, that is precisely where the ball goes.

The third hitter meets with the same result. Riseball, riseball, riseball. No resorting to any sort of pitching trickery like a changeup or some other kind of off-speed pitch. "Here comes my fastball, you think you can hit it?," is the question. "Let's find out," is the challenge.

The fourth batter stands in and, like his teammates, sees three 100 mph pitches go by from a distance of 46 feet. I don't remember whether he tried to swing at any of them. I do remember that wherever Carl Solarek put the glove, Ty Stofflet put the ball.

It was mesmerizing, and it answered any questions that I had about what the best looked like. I went down to the field and said something like, "Great game." He thanked me. I then asked him how he held the riser. He apologized for not being able to show me the pitch from the sidelines, but he put the ball into his hands and told me how to release it. He ended by saying, "It will take about two years to get it right." He offered to show me more if I came to another Reading game, and I thanked him.

For those of you who have never seen Ty Stofflet actually grip a softball to throw a riser, it looks like a pitch that

Prologue

would hurt to throw, mainly because it is a pitch that hurts to throw. The ball is jammed into the middle three fingers looking like a snow cone. I tried the pitch following the Poughkeepsie game but gave it up because the stretch it put on the webbing of my fingers caused some pain. Much later I found out that Ty had arthritis in four fingers of his left hand, which also made the riser hurt him through the first few innings of a game. Once the fingers became numb, they didn't hurt for the remainder of that game. We both felt pain; he had figured out a way not to mind.

The next time I saw Ty and the Sunners was in 1979, just around the time he was featured in *Sports Illustrated*. My New Jersey team played a tournament in Lancaster, PA, and the 1977, 1978 national champion Sunners were playing in our bracket. I was one of four pitchers on our team and had no particular interest in facing them. Both Sammy Ardolino and Jimmy Prayer wanted the game. But our manager, in an effort to show that he wasn't playing favorites (we had no ace as yet), decided to give the ball to me, the third pitcher.

It was a filler game for the Sunners, a way to keep active through the summer in between games versus the better competition. For four innings, the game was scoreless. But we were never in the game. Ronnie Kist, who was now our New Jersey team catcher, got a first-inning bunt single and you could almost feel the relief going through our bench. It was that palpable. Today we would not become another no-hitter notched into Ty's career statistics. Nobody else had even a loud foul ball throughout the game, however, as Ty went methodically through the lineup.

At the time we were the best team in New Jersey. The team later went on to represent New Jersey in four "AA" (major) ASA nationals. In 1984, five of our players joined

Softball's Lefty Legend ~ Ty Stofflet

Santilli and the Sunners, and stayed with them for three years, but today we were just the opponent of the moment.

Because of the special rules of this tournament, no game was allowed to exceed seven innings. Perhaps a tie would be possible. In the fifth inning, however, the Sunners scored a run. Two innings later Jeff Seip hit a tape measure shot that jumped out of the park almost before I could turn around to see where it went. On paper it was a four-hit, two-run loss on my part. In reality, we never got to be a blip on the radar screen.

Ronnie and I have talked about the connection that New Jersey players feel they have with Ty. Kist is a perceptive, wry guy who has an educator's way of getting to the heart of the matter. "Look Doc," he said to me somewhere near a ball field, "Ty is the combination of Michael Jordan and Babe Ruth to our sport. There isn't anything that a player should do on the diamond that he can't do better than almost anybody who played the game. And people love to see him play."

Many years after Ronnie and I had retired, I asked him if he knew anyone who could teach my daughter, Sarah, to throw windmill. He gave me Ty's phone number with a confident smile as he said, "Ty's a peach of a guy."

That brings us to an indoor batting cage outside of Coplay, PA, where Ty lives. He treats me with the respect that any four-star softball general would give a civilian. We are on his turf and my task is to crouch behind the plate and catch my daughter's pitches. His job is to concentrate on the new "hurler" from New Jersey.

Right from the start, Ty was a combination of enthusiasm and focus. His philosophy started with the idea that the girls he taught needed to like their teacher or they wouldn't heed any of his lessons. It was his job to come to

Prologue

them emotionally, not vice versa. Whatever else was going to be part of Sarah's softball training, she was going to have fun during the lessons.

Ty quickly developed rapport with his student. From my position, 40 feet away behind home plate, it was easy to see that student and mentor were enjoying each other's company. There were lots of laughs all around. However, life is not a free ride and Ty quickly added the idea that students who worked at their craft between lessons made the most progress in the shortest amount of time.

Once Sarah demonstrated that she was willing to practice between lessons, Ty made himself personally available in case this girl coming from New Jersey had any questions. Thus, the second philosophical message stood out in bold detail. Talent is interesting for its potential, but focused practice and intelligent rehearsal enable the thrower to evolve into a pitcher.

As Ty articulated necessary steps to a winning profile, it became obvious that he was describing a set of quality of life strategies imbedded in a recipe for on and off the field success. He taught the value of thinking, planning and anticipating, as much as he taught the value of having a reliable release point for each pitch. There was no sense in having the tools if you didn't know how to make the best use of them.

As the second phase of the lessons was put in place, Ty became the insider whose world of softball experience might one day take his student to anyplace she could imagine. Here the focus of the lessons shifted to the "smarts of the game" and both daughter and father got to listen to one of the game's top talents engage in a master class for one. Surprisingly, the master was as interested in the welfare of his pupil's team as he was in the productivity of the individual. Being smart meant being smart at a number of levels. Social intelligence was demonstrated by how much respect and cooperation each player shared with her teammates.

At precisely that moment, this quality of life psychologist saw an opportunity for a collaboration that might provide some insights to others concerned about how the quest to be the best can remain consistent with the need to be a productive part of the community.

Having gotten to know the person through his role as teacher, I knew he had a treasure trove of information about this game that deserved to be shared. In researching the events of his career, more and more aspects surfaced that demanded to be told.

First, in the words of the old adage, "He came to play." The single word used most to describe him by his peers was "prepared." No one can remember a time when he came to a ball field mentally, emotionally or physically unprepared to do his best.

Second, on the softball diamond he could be counted on to be the most confident man in the world at that particular moment. That confidence was a source of inspiration to his teammates, but not a source of resentment to his opponents, because he was careful. He expected to strike out the side every inning of every game, but without any show or even a hint of bad sportsmanship.

Third, the bigger the stage, the better was the performance. My own guess is that because Ty was never a bully, his true enjoyment came in facing those who came to the plate with a plan. His prodigious talent was best served during those times when he was forced to turn on the afterburners and use all his skills to defeat their plan.

Fourth: concentration, concentration, concentration.

Prologue

Of the five catchers interviewed for this project, each marveled at his ability to concentrate one pitch at a time for as long as a game or a tournament might last. His team might lose a game while he was pitching, but it wouldn't be because his mind was somewhere else.

Fifth, Ty is the quintessential team player. He has a gregarious makeup and has too much fun around people to be anything else. He has made it a point to make anybody on his side of the field as comfortable as possible throughout his career. And once a game has been decided, no hard feelings, win or lose. He calls it respect, but it is respect with a twinkle of the eye, and it says it's okay to have fun – in the end it's only a game.

Profile of a Softball Legend

The Early Years

"The Ferocious Gentleman"

THE GAME OF FAST PITCH softball is fast, but it is anything but soft. Most men who played both hardball and softball will tell you that they felt at least as physically at risk playing softball as they did playing hardball. True, a hardball is harder than a softball, but believe it or not, the top softball pitchers get to stand about 15 feet closer to the batter while being able to throw the ball at least as fast as the best Major League hardball pitchers.

As far as the other defensive players are concerned, the 60 feet between bases in softball places a premium on all players' abilities to react with enormous quickness. Men who played professional baseball in minor league organizations and later made their way to "AA" fast pitch are quick to cite the need for additional quickness and precision that comes with the transition from hardball to softball.

All of the infielders interviewed in the preparation of this book – many of whom were professional Minor League baseball players before becoming All-American softball players – pointed out that baseball is a more forgiving sport than softball when it comes to bobbled balls. Their summary thought on the matter of quickness was, "You have a little time to make up for a bobble in baseball because of the greater distance to first base. In softball either field it cleanly and make a quick accurate throw, or just hand it back to the pitcher."

In his prime, Ty Stofflet was the personification of softball swiftness. In fact, his world of softball greatness

Softball's Lefty Legend ~ Ty Stofflet

was covered in *The New York Times Sunday Magazine* under the title, "*The Fastest Pitcher in America* (August 11, 1985)," when he was 44. In the May 28, 1979, issue of *Sports Illustrated*, a feature article about Ty also got to the heart of the matter in its title, "*This Guy Can Rise It, Drop it, and Pop It at 104 MPH.*"

For those of you who might be wondering just how the 104.7 mph was established, it was done by means of a tracking mechanism set up at home plate 46 feet away from the originally pitched ball. The thrown ball had to pass through the inside of the target in order for an accurate velocity to be recorded.

Physicists will tell you that the ball actually leaves the pitcher's hand at a somewhat higher velocity than is recorded at home plate. Air friction is responsible for the slow down. Today, handheld radar guns typically record the speed of a ball when it leaves the pitcher's hand. In other words, if today's recording equipment had been available at the time of the *Sport's Illustrated* article, it would probably have measured Ty's speed at his release point at about 106 mph.

Such was Ty's fame that a brief exhibition against Major League players was staged on television in 1978 on *The Dick Clark Show.* Davey Lopes, Reggie Smith and Steve Yaeger agreed to face Ty and his catcher, Carl Solarek, at Dodger Stadium. Even though the batters were established Major Leaguers just returning from the World Series against the Yankees, a foul tip against Ty Stofflet was considered a victory.

The softball is bigger than a hardball and therefore seemingly easier to hit, but the underhand delivery and larger ball surface makes it possible for the skilled pitcher to move it in all directions. (That's right – up, down and

"The Ferocious Gentleman"

sideways.) A baseball pitcher with enormous velocity can get the ball to "hop" or rise a number of inches. A riseball pitcher, however, who generates the right spin from the underhand release point, can get a softball to jump upward more that a foot and a half on its trip to home plate.

In both baseball and softball general rules of thumb help determine the outcomes of individual games. Generally speaking, great hitting beats good pitching, but more times than not, great pitching beats great hitting. All great hitters rely on a pitching mistake that may be just a ball width away from where the pitcher intended it to go.

One of the things that separates the "best" from the rest, is that the best very seldom make that mistake, and they almost never do it during moments when the game is on the line. Rather, they somehow find a way to pick their game up a notch and become even faster or exhibit even better movement and finer control during these pivotal moments.

After all of my interviews with players, managers and officials of the game who saw Ty play, it is safe to make this summary statement. He was the most consistently excellent ballplayer they could remember ever being around. Some players, like one of his long-time catchers, Carl Solarek, described it as a "work ethic." "I played against pitchers who could keep up with Ty for most of a game, or could even throw a game that approached perfection, but they couldn't duplicate that effort for the next game. Ty could and did."

Solarek caught Ty for about a decade in more than 500 games. According to him, Ty's work ethic was such that he could will himself to concentrate fully on every single pitch of every single inning in every single game. Everyone who saw him compete on a softball field repeat-

Softball's Lefty Legend ~ Ty Stofflet

ed that observation. Those who saw him play could all define times when he personally "put the game on his back" and went into a higher playing gear, but nobody ever saw him give less than his best.

As articles noted above from *The New York Times* and *Sports Illustrated* suggest, Ty had the ability to make the crossover from being a member of his sport to being a recognized standard bearer for it. With the exceptions of Eddie Feigner, barnstorming with The King and His Court, and Joan Joyce, who also demonstrated crossover appeal, Ty was the fast pitch player who defined his sport for the general public. And since The King and His Court was a source of entertainment rather than a model of sanctioned rule-bound softball, Ty's role as the public face of organized softball was unique in his sport.

I am certain that it was Ty's talent and popularity on the softball field that resulted in an offer by Mr. Feigner to join The King and His Court, to which the *Sports Illustrated* article alluded. Given what I have learned about Ty and his values, I do not believe that there was a price that would have proved acceptable to turn him into an itinerant traveler. Particularly, for a man who has chosen to live his adult life right next door to his father and mother.

It is well accepted that Ty had the potential to be a lethal person from the proximity of a 46-foot pitching distance. It is as reliably documented that he never used that form of intimidation. Batters who spoke to me, including Hall of Famers who faced him in national competitions, described him as tough but not mean. That is code for the fact that they knew that Ty would not purposely throw at their bodies. He might, on the occasion of some wildness, hit them, but he would never intentionally hurt them.

That story is reminiscent of how baseball players

"The Ferocious Gentleman"

described what it was like to face the legendary baseball lefty, Sandy Koufax. It was sufficiently terrifying to stand there at the plate against a man who threw around a 100 mph. Knowing that he might be a head hunter could add something to the game that might turn a contest into blood sport. Neither Koufax nor Stofflet needed that sort of life-changing event on his conscience. In the end, it just wasn't worth it.

Ty grew up in a Pennsylvania Dutch family, proud of their heritage. The family was, is and will always be close because they invest the time and effort to remain in contact. Father, Harold, and mother, Melba, raised three children, an older daughter, Lillian, their first son, Ty, and his one-year-younger brother, Larry. This is a church-going family that held gatherings without fail every Sunday afternoon for about 20 years.

Another area of family fervor that Harold passed on to his sons and daughter was the love of ball playing. Harold Stofflet was both a baseball and softball pitcher in and around Allentown. When the children were old enough to come to any ballpark where he was playing, he would have them travel with him and sit on the bench with the players.

By the time Ty was 10, he was making his first attempts to try the new motion, windmill, although his dad was a figure-eight thrower. When the boys were 13 and 14, Harold put them on his team rosters in case there weren't enough players for a particular game. There were times when both boys got to play, and they played well enough to want to continue.

But to get a real sense of Harold's intense interest in his childrens' ball playing, ask him why both of his sons throw the ball left-handed and his daughter throws both lefty

Softball's Lefty Legend ~ Ty Stofflet

and righty. As early in their lives as he could, Harold put all balls in the kid's left hand. "I did it because I really loved the way Lefty Grove (the Hall of Fame lefty baseball pitcher) threw the ball."

What is interesting is that Harold is clearly going against the grain. Most parents and teachers at that time went out of their way to discourage left-handed preferences, whether handwriting or other skills, instead patterning right-handed behavior. Harold Stofflet felt differently and worked at creating two lefty sons. He maintains that he did not do the same with their hitting – both hit left-handed, but he is very clear about establishing a lefty preference for their throwing.

Larry is the family member who during his career looked the image of the 6'2", 240-pound player who dwarfed his older, thinner brother. Both learned to throw, and to this day Ty does not understand why his brother didn't also pursue a pitching career. "He was fast," said Ty on numerous occasions, "almost as fast as I was. He could have been great if he had worked on it."

Larry, for his part, speaks about softball as a true hitter, the rest of the game being necessary only so that you can get to hit again. "My brother is a perfectionist," says Larry Stofflet. "Give him a chance to work on anything that matters to him like pitching, hitting, fielding, running, ping pong, bowling and horseshoes. With enough time, he will learn all about the game and practice, practice, practice until he gets good enough at it to beat anybody."

Larry could not see what all the fuss was about. Ty can't see how anybody could miss the opportunity to be the best at anything they have a chance to be best at. This is definitely a situation where opposites make for compatible family harmony. The bigger of the two brothers, who hap-

Ty, Larry & Lillian - 1946

Melba & Harold Stofflet

"The Ferocious Gentleman"

pens to be younger, is less internally competitive than his older brother. They do a lot of playing together but their purpose is fun and personal improvement. It is not the destruction of the enemy.

Larry tells a tale about times when they were learning to throw windmill and were pitching to each other. "We would spend an hour throwing to each other, 15 minutes throwing and 45 minutes retrieving the ball." He also tells a story about Ty's control at that time, and the family chicken coop out in the back. "We would throw with the chicken coop as a backstop. Dad would come home and see holes in the wall made by softballs. He made a little fuss, but not too much."

Harold Stofflet remembers the chicken coop incident a little bit differently. "The boys went to the back and broke a few windows in the chicken coop, so I showed them how to repair the damage they had caused by learning to fix the windows. After making the repairs, their control improved quickly."

Listen to Larry and you get the idea that the brothers found as many ways as they could to create games against each other with as many different kinds of balls as they had in their possession. To this day, Ty credits his early pitching and hitting games with Larry as making him a better hitter. Larry, in turn, reminds his listener that he was both Ty's first catcher and the one who caught more pitches from his brother than anyone else.

Early in his life, when it became obvious that Ty had been graced with the gift of extraordinary speed, his father had this frank conversation with his son. "If you ever seriously hurt a player from the mound, the game will be over for you," instructed his father. "Everybody works for a living at something besides softball. Don't ever put another man's livelihood in jeopardy."

Softball's Lefty Legend ~ Ty Stofflet

Harold Stofflet also shaped Ty's mental, emotional and social approaches to the game. According to Ty, his father believes strongly that each of us has a duty to make the most of the skills given to us. When Harold saw the raw skills possessed by his son, he planted the seed that Ty might just imagine growing up to be the best in the game. Not just a regional or national best, but the best that his generation produced.

As intimidating as those words may have sounded to a 14-year-old, who never ventured far from Allentown, PA, they were also inspiring and goal-setting. From his vantage point near the ball fields of his hometown, he could watch visitors like the Clearwater Bombers come to town and experience the vicarious thrills of what it would be like to become a top-notch softball barnstormer like Hall of Famer Johnny Spring. More important, he could get up close and personal, asking these major pitchers how they spun their magic. "It was just a bike ride away, and I made that trip often," says Ty. "They were the ones I wanted to study and learn from."

Okay. So this far into Ty's history we know that his dad has introduced the idea of personal softball greatness in his son's mind. It is easy to imagine a kid who is throwing super fast and contemplating personal greatness, who quickly develops a set of superior airs, especially when he considered himself on track to possibly be compared to a Johnny Spring.

Here is where Harold Stofflet sets himself apart from the common variety parent of a precocious young man. According to Ty, his dad makes it clear that softball is a team game played by gentlemen. While he may have superior physical skills, he is no better as a human being than anyone he plays with or against. In fact, the measure of his skills as a player must always include efforts to help boost

"The Ferocious Gentleman"

his teammates no matter how they played.

Stand near Ty for even a short period and you will hear the word "respect." For him, it is something that one gives others, not as a gift but as their right. It may be perfectly acceptable between the lines of play to take advantage of every possible weakness presented by your opponent. It is never acceptable to do anything that might be interpreted as poor sportsmanship, no matter the level of bush play others might attempt.

When asked about what they remembered most, traveling throughout the country during the summers with their mom, Kathy, and their dad, daughters Kim, Brenda and Kris told a story that at first surprised me, but later fit into the general scope of information I had been collecting from other parties.

It seems that a team, which will remain nameless and which, like many other teams, had not experienced recent success against him, was facing Ty and the Sunners in a holiday tournament. Some team members hatched a plan. At the end of their defensive half inning, and before Ty came out to the mound, they threw a tainted rosin bag (one containing an illegal substance, usually some rock rosin instead of the legal powdered rosin) behind the pitcher's mound. When Ty began to take his warmups, they went to the umpire claiming that Ty should be tossed from the game because he was cheating. The ploy didn't work.

What the ladies remembered nearly 20 years later was their dad's reaction in the car on the way home. "They had a good enough team to have a chance to beat me on the field. Why try to hurt someone else's reputation to get something that's not worth the effort?" The other team had violated Ty's most sacred rule for all competitors, "Win fairly or don't waste your time."

Softball's Lefty Legend ~ Ty Stofflet

According to his daughters, the trip home was highlighted by their father's explanation of the relative importance of a softball victory. While it was good to win a tough game, in the end it was only a game. Softball players who forgot that fact ran the risk of losing their moral footing. Each of his children retained vivid memories of the event because of how hurt (not angry) their dad was by the unsavory tactic. "He just couldn't understand what would make a talented group of people behave that way. It showed no respect for the game, themselves or us."

And so we have another Stofflet premise about life and softball. In the grand scheme of things there is one's faith, one's family, and one's community. As long as the games are played according to rules that respect this hierarchy, enjoy the competition and be as tough as the rules allow. Go beyond the lines of decency and something of value is forever lost. When all is said and done, the moral rudder establishes the basis for a solid journey through life.

The astute reader is asking an obvious question by now, "What about baseball?" Simply put, Ty thought it was slow, and aesthetically unpleasing. He never saw much use for it and didn't give it much time or effort. Even when the Philadelphia Phillies wanted him to join them as a submariner, he gave it a perfunctory attempt, and came to the conclusion that his ball showed too little movement. Besides, he could unduly jeopardize his softball eligibility if he attempted a hardball pitching career

Earlier, Ty's trip to face several Dodgers in 1978 at the height of the Sunners' domination of fast pitch softball was mentioned. We already alluded to the fact that the Dodgers had a hard time getting a piece of the ball. However, there is more. At the conclusion of the exhibition, as Davey Lopes and Ty started talking, Lopes asked him where he

"The Ferocious Gentleman"

was heading next. "It sounded to me like he thought that this television exhibition was part of a country-wide tour. I told him that I was returning to my job at Mack Trucks as an electrician. He looked at me in disbelief and said, pointing to my left arm, 'With an arm like that, you work for a living?'"

Some artists work in oil paints, others work in watercolors, and still others chip marble until the sculpture is drawn from the stone. Ty Stofflet was born to be a softball legend, apparently not a baseball one. In addition to his hitting prowess, however, if you add the fact that he was one of the fastest runners on any team he played for, had extraordinary reflexes, and was one of the few softball pitchers who also had a top-notch overhand throwing motion, there is certainly some room to speculate about his chances as a hardball player.

To further understand Ty's preference for softball over hardball it might be helpful to know that the Allentown-Reading-Lehigh Valley Region of Pennsylvania was a stronghold of softball activity. The church league in which he started pitching at 17 had about 18 teams. The Allentown City League had divisions of teams as did the industrial competition. Nearly everywhere you looked in 1958, somebody was playing fast pitch softball.

At 17, Ty plays in the church league and, according to his brother, is so wild they would allow him to pitch until he started to hit batters, and when it became dangerous, they would move him to another position.

He stays in the church league, improving his control for the next few years, until at 21, Earl Hunsicker, Allentown Patriots' owner/manager, notices him. Earl, through his automobile workers' union connections, is able to procure jobs for Ty and Larry at Mack Trucks. Both

Softball's Lefty Legend ~ Ty Stofflet

Ty and Larry acknowledge that Earl found them jobs with one of the best benefits packages in the area. The brothers remained at Mack Trucks for their entire working careers.

In 1963, Ty and Larry Stofflet join the Allentown Patriots; Ty as a pitcher, and Larry as a first baseman/right fielder. Hunsicker at this time is a serious softball team owner who is in the process of developing Patriots Park, a softball field that will go through continuous building improvements for the next 30-plus years. Earl is also the driving force behind Bicentennial Park, completed in 1976, and which was posthumously named after him in recognition of his contributions to all phases of its development.

In 1963, the Patriots have a goal: to win the K.A.S.A. Pennsylvania State Championship and earn the right to go to the ISC World Championship in Rock Island, IL. According to team catcher, Phil Schantz, "Earl had a formula for going into tournaments in those days. He would start a game with Ty on the mound and me behind the plate. If we needed more than one win that day, he would put us out in the field as soon as our team got ahead and put us back if we needed to stop the other team from scoring. Mickey Hoffman would catch and Dick Bingell would pitch and see if they could hold the lead for us."

Just such a day is described in the Allentown Patriots' 25th year Anniversary Program and also recalled by Phil Schantz. "We are in the losers' bracket on the final day of the state tournament. We need four wins that day, but Earl comes in and says, 'We have to win a single, 28-inning game. All we have to do is be ahead at the end of seven innings, 14 innings, 21 innings and 28 innings and the tournament is ours.'"

Schantz goes on to say that he and Ty spent the 100-

"The Ferocious Gentleman"

degree day as battery mates and switching back and forth from the battery to playing in the field. Ty remembers that day with these thoughts, "I'm glad it happened when I was young. As I got older I never would have been able to change positions like that. It would have killed my concentration."

The Patriots go to Rock Island, IL, and get their first taste of ISC competition. "I'll never forget just how intimidating it was," said Schantz. "I don't think that Ty was fully ready either. He didn't warm up with enough pitches. The other team scores a run in the first, but by the second inning we know that we can play with these guys. We lose that game, 1-0." From the record kept by the ISC, Ty pitched 10 innings in that tournament, struck out 19, allowed five hits and walked six. The team goes 0-2 that year.

In 1964, the Pates also win the state championship qualifier that sends them to the ISC World Championship, held again in Rock Island, IL. By now they have become a local force, winning the City Softball League and the East Penn Major Softball League. At the 1964 ISC World Championship, Ty and his team are much better prepared. Stofflet has a 2-2 record in 29 2/3 innings, again according to official ISC statistics, with five walks, 48 strikeouts and two earned runs in four games.

That year, at 23, Ty receives a special award. He is voted Most Popular Player and receives a radio for his trophy case. The Patriots win the ISC World Tournament Sportsmanship Award, also in 1964. The composition of the ISC in those days, according to Royce Heath, ISC Hall of Famer, consisted of 23 teams from all over the USA and Canada. Each team either won a qualifier, like the Pates, or came in first in an ISC travel league. The team from

Softball's Lefty Legend ~ Ty Stofflet

Allentown is showing that it belongs in this tournament in more ways than one.

Heath identified that Ty was the MVP in six straight ISC qualifying tournaments over the period 1964-69. But Ty Stofflet thrives on competitive goals, and a pattern develops. It was never his intention to stand still. By the second year of any personal achievement, you can be sure that he is focused on bringing his team to the next level.

In 1965, the Patriots again qualify for the ISC World Championships with Ty as their KASA MVP. The team garners third place in the tournament and Ty's record is 4-2. He pitches 41 2/3 innings with a comparatively low 47 strikeouts. Third is respectable because the team has never gotten to third before. It is a far cry from first. This year and the next, Allentown wins the ISC World Tournament Sportsmanship Award.

In 1966, all the previous team high water marks are hit going into the ISC World Championship. The Pates are KASA state champs with all the local awards. Ty is again 4-2 as his team finishes fourth in the ISC World Tournament. For the first time in international competition, he has struck out less than one per inning (34 strikeouts in 37 2/3 innings). He has also given up slightly more than one earned run per game in both 1965 and 1966.

To make some sense of these statistics, it's useful to go back to Phil Schantz, Ty's first major catcher. "In the early years," said Phil, "Ty was just a flamethrower with a riser and a flat curve. I never caught him in a crouch, that ball moved so much at 100 mph. Most of the time, I caught the ball above my head after the batter had swung at something around his chest. There was no changeup to speak of."

Larry, Ty & Harold, Church League - 1958

Warming up with the Church Team - 1960

"The Ferocious Gentleman"

Ty, in the meantime, is learning at a rapid rate. At the ISC level of play, he will have to come to town with more than a straight curve and a riser or they will marvel at his speed and send his team home a loser every year. Fortunately, living in a universe of softball players of every category and description, he has had the opportunity to make decisions regarding what will be needed to complete his pitching array. He develops a drop, thrown about 15 miles slower than the riser, and a changeup thrown about 15 miles slower than the drop.

You might suspect that there is a lot of ego that plays back and forth between the top-notch pitcher and top-notch hitter. The hitter can't be equally ready for every pitch that is about to be thrown. And the limit of human reaction time is already stretched by the demands of a 100+ mph pitch that moves more than a foot upward on its way to the plate. Add two other pitches and the hitter is now left to guess even before the pitch is released.

Jim Brackin, a Hall of Fame shortstop who played with and against Ty, described the dilemma as follows: "No good hitter wants to be late on the fastball. It's a matter of pride. Ty's fastball was so fast that his other pitches were back breakers. The top batters' mindset was, 'Don't get beat on the fastball,' so we looked silly on the slow stuff."

It is in 1967 that Ty is ready to assume his place in the pantheon of top softball pitchers and players. We also have the benefit of the ISC 1968 program (courtesy of Floyd Hammen of the ISC Hall of Fame) which describes Ty's 1967 accomplishments in specific detail. In the first game, Ty strikes out 15 as Allentown beats Lamar, CO, 2-0. In the second game against the home team, Rock Island Sport Shop, Ty strikes out 18 on his way to a perfect game.

Softball's Lefty Legend ~ Ty Stofflet

According to the account, "None of the first nine batters touched the ball and nobody hit it out of the infield."

The next game against Lakewood, CA, lasts 16 innings, as Ty gets a complete game win, 2-1. A portent of things to come, Ty hits an RBI triple in the fifth to tie the game and is out stretching it into an inside-the-park-home run. The play at home has him diving headfirst. In 12 innings, Harrelson Motors of Moline beats the Patriots, 4-0. The article mentions a terrific catch by brother Larry as well, to keep the game tied at 0-0.

The Patriots win their next game, 5-2, as Ty is beginning to show some tiredness on the mound. Of course, that didn't stop him from hitting a bases-loaded triple in the third inning to put away the game. That puts the Pates back into the finals against Dick Brubaker, the pitcher from Moline who was inducted into the ISC Hall of Fame along with Ty in 1984.

Ty is a sentimental choice for the fans, although he is not expected to get through the Moline team. He goes three innings and strikes out his 83rd, 84th, and 85th batters in the third inning to give him the ISC World Tournament record. He is taken out in the fourth inning.

In Murry Hart's concluding comments for the 1968 review of the 1967 ISC World Championship (pgs. 10-11), he notes: "But even defeat couldn't dim the luster of Stofflet's tournament performance. He pitched 52 innings – 38 over the last three days – gave up just one earned run, entered a perfect game into the record books, set a tournament strikeout record with 85, and just for good measure batted an even .300."

Hart went on to say, "One of the most coveted individual awards for tournament players is the Most Popular Player trophy. If anyone doubted Stofflet's credentials

Ty in 1964 ISC World Championship

Ty scoring in 1964 ISC World Champsioinship

Larry Stofflet scores in 1964 ISC World Championship

Ty & Larry win first ISC World Tournament game – 1964

Most Popular Player Trophy - 1964 ISC World Championship

Softball's Lefty Legend ~ Ty Stofflet

before the final night, the doubts were erased when the fans gave him an ear-shattering standing ovation when he left the hill in the fourth inning of the title game.

He also won the Most Valuable Player award – a unanimous vote – and, of course, was selected to head the mound staff on the All-World squad."

Welcome to the top echelon of ISC individual achievements. But by now you have probably guessed that second place creates an itch that Ty must scratch, no matter the individual laurels. It is at this point that Ty takes his game to the big city, Philadelphia, PA, and joins Sal's Lunch, a team looking for a pitcher to take them to the top.

This is a controversial move, particularly from the perspective of the average Allentown Patriots' fan, but without him ever saying so, I must conclude that the 26-year-old phenom wants to see what softball life will be like from the vantage point of the larger venue. His direct quote on the matter is, "They always treated me very well in Philly. I wanted to see if I could help them win a championship."

In the 1968 ISC World Championship Ty's record is 3-1. He strikes out 71 in 34 innings, with four walks, gives up one run (it is earned) in four games, bats .333 (6 for 18), and is the MVP in the tournament, according to the 1984 ISC World Tournament program. Although the report for 1968 is sketchy, things have worked well enough for Ty to decide to play a second year with Sal's Lunch. It is that second year which remains in record books to the present time.

In the 1969 ISC World Tournament, Sal's Lunch bats 19th out of 24 teams, with a .151 team batting average. Their leadoff hitter, Ty Stofflet, hits .294 (5 for 17). The team scores a total of seven runs in five games, and still manages to win all five games to win the tournament.

"The Ferocious Gentleman"

For the record, Sal's Lunch of Philadelphia stays in the winners' bracket with a first-game win over Van Wert of OH, 1-0. They break out for three runs against Hawthorn, CA, 3-0, in their second game. They next beat host Bob Neal, 1-0, followed by a 1-0 win over the Rock Island Sport Shop.

In the final game against The Sport Shop, Ty throws a one-hit shutout and gets two of his team's four hits. Sal's Lunch scores an unearned run in the second inning and breezes along on Ty's near perfect pitching. He loses a perfect game in the sixth on a walk and a no-hitter with two out in the seventh on a single to right.

Records achieved during this tournament include an ERA of 0.00 in 42 innings. That combined with the last 2 1/3 scoreless innings from the previous year give him 44 1/3 consecutive scoreless innings over the 1968-69 seasons. During this tournament, he adds a no-hitter along with his final game one-hitter and strikes out 86 in 42 innings. In 10 fewer innings than he pitched in 1967, he has struck out one more batter. Ty captures another MVP, and once again makes the All-World team.

The itch has been scratched in a way that puts an exclamation point on the first part of his ISC World Championship career. During the next 14 years, because of jurisdictional disputes between the ASA and the ISC, Ty will not be allowed to play in further ISC World Tournaments while he chases ASA aspirations.

One can speculate about how many additional games he might have won during the years 1970-1983, but the facts are facts. With the fruition of ISC championship aspirations, Ty now turns his attention to returning to legal ASA player status.

In the meanwhile, the ISC has proved to be a worthy stage for this young man with lofty ambitions. He has

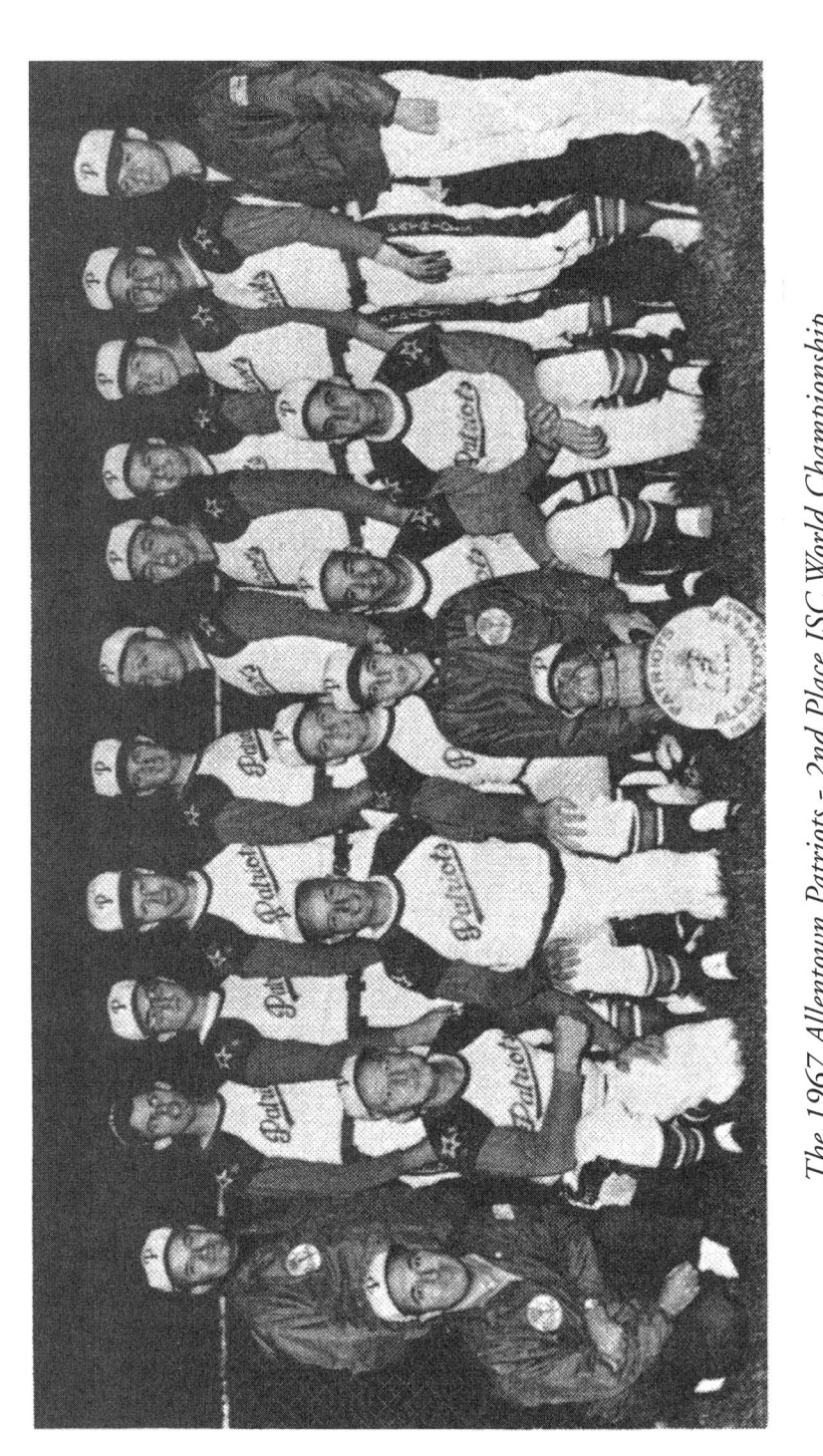

The 1967 Allentown Patriots - 2nd Place ISC World Championship. Harold (top left), Ty, top row, 4th from right, Larry, top row, 3rd from right.

"The Ferocious Gentleman"

solved the problem of how to face top echelon hitting during his seven years of ISC competition, while he has adapted to the realities of low run production and long, tension-filled games.

This is also the stage of his career when he establishes the all-tools qualities of his game. Now that he approaches accomplished hitters with a full arsenal of pitching choices, he is free to rely on the creative artistry that will mark his career for the next 23 years of top flight competition.

At the same time, there is now an obvious rapport between Ty and softball enthusiasts wherever he goes. He enjoys a large crowd and is able to use the spirit of the crowd to help him pitch a little better. He has also discovered that the bigger the stage and the more at stake in the game, the better he can find his competitive edge. They may not know him yet in the ASA bastions of softball competition, but he intends to change that.

1969 Sal's Lunch - 1st place ISC World Championship. Ty bottom row, left, with certificate.

The Sunners

The Quest to be the Best

Making Connections

LEESPORT, PA, SEEMS AN unlikely location for the birthplace of a fast pitch softball dynasty. It is about 45 minutes southwest of Allentown, and within 10 miles of Reading. A visit to Rocky and Ginny Santilli's home in the spring takes you past small farms with cornfields being readied for the new season. Drivers let each other into line and people who honk their horns at one another are just as likely to be saying, "Hello," as they are to be expressing some impatience.

Rocky Santilli, 77 years old, coaches the local high school girls' softball team. Ever since he was 30 years old he has been a softball coach in and around Reading and Allentown. A series of back injuries have clearly slowed him down, but given a little time to settle into his recreation room amid a cache of team trophies, he can be persuaded to talk about how a team gathered almost completely from a 28-mile area got to become national and international champions.

When I first saw Rocky about 25 years ago, I remember him as a barrel-chested big man who stood about five and a half feet tall, give or take. Softball managers come in two forms, those who run their team and those who allow the team to run them. Rocky ran his team and, by behavior and demeanor, made that fact clear to anyone who cared to notice.

Rocky described the personal code by which he had managed others through his 40 years of coaching. A story he tells about himself summarizes his bottom line philosophy regarding whom to play. "I was a catcher who was self taught. Very good defensively, but just good offensively. When I was 34, we had the chance to pick up a fellow who was coming out of the Detroit Tigers organization. He was a catcher, and so he took my job behind the plate."

Bill Miller, my coach in New Jersey in the mid '80s, had become Rocky's friend in part because Rocky had been willing to help Bill figure out what he needed to do to manage his New Jersey team. I am not sure just how many others made the trek to Leesport to seek Rocky's advice, but you can bet that Bill was not alone.

Bill improved his team by adding better players until one day he, too, acquired the means to make himself obsolete. To their credit, both men saw the acquisition of better talent as their primary responsibility and refused to shirk that responsibility even if it meant losing their place as an active player on their own team.

As a player on a team whose manager behaved according to this script, I could always count on the guy's fairness. I didn't necessarily have to agree with his selections, but I knew that the team could count on his integrity. Tom Wagner, the Hall of Fame manager of Pay 'n Pak from Seattle, WA, fully agrees with this form of team government. "It is always a good idea to let the players know just who has the final say about team decisions. If they don't like it, they always have the choice to play for someone else."

Rocky considers himself a good and objective source of softball talent. Because he was restricted by budget through most of his coaching years, he made it a point to get to know the best athletes in his region and showed considerable imagination regarding where to place them in the

Making Connections

defensive lineup. "Did you know that our starting lineup that appeared in the 1974 national contained seven shortstops? When they came to the Sunners, I moved them to a position that would best help the team have a chance to win."

There must be something about the water in Berks and Lehigh counties in Pennsylvania that contributes to congenial, friendly team play. Maybe it's because Rocky scouted his personnel well, weeding out troublemakers. Or perhaps the team's years of local success during the '60s created faith in Rocky's methods. Whatever the combination of reasons, Rocky had his team convinced that they were improving every year. With a few more pieces of the puzzle, they could go on to the nationals instead of being sent home from the regionals year after year.

If you talk to Bob Yoder, Joe Lalli or Jerry Heist who played with the Sunners before Ty came in 1970, they tell a tale of "almost" or "not quite." "There seemed to be enough talent at all positions, but somehow either Flatiron, or Baltimore or Fox Hill would go to the nationals for the 10 years prior to 1971," according to Rocky. "As well as they played to win the regionals, none of those teams seemed to do very well in the nationals."

And so, here are the Sunners, a local team with the best talent that Rocky can find, looking for some glue that will hold the pieces together.

The Weekend from Hell

SO, YOU WANT TO BE THE ACE of your softball team? In both baseball and softball terminology, the team's ace is the pitcher counted on to win any and all games that matter. In baseball, the team finds a way to schedule the ace to throw the big game and then rest for about four days before throwing another. In softball the ace is expected to throw one, two or even more than two games in the same day.

In Pennsylvania the reigning champion of the title "rubber armed ace" is George Ulmer, who in 1970 is playing with Flatiron. Rocky Santilli remembers. "We faced him in a regional tournament where we watched him start the day by winning a 21-inning game. Later that same day he lost a seven-inning game to us and immediately came back to win the next game against us." What matters here is not just that Ulmer just pitched five games worth of innings in the same day, but that he was effective enough to win the last one.

Jimmy Moore, the Hall of Fame ace of Pay 'n Pak during the '80s, described being an ace in this way. "The ace gets the ball whenever the team needs a win. The ace is always ready to come into any game at any time. If need be, the ace might pitch every game of the tournament, no matter how many other pitchers are available."

Moore went on to explain that the best teams have a second pitcher who is slightly below the level of the ace. That second pitcher usually starts the second game of scheduled doubleheaders, and may even fill in for the ace. However, to deserve the title, each ace expects to bear the lion's share of the pitching burden.

In order to understand just how Ty and his fellow Sunners came together during 1970, it is important to understand just how double elimination tournaments are constructed. In every double elimination tournament, there are two brackets. Every team starts out in the winners' bracket. At the conclusion of every game, there is a winner and a loser. The winner remains in the winners' bracket, the loser moves to the "dreaded" losers' bracket.

There are a number of things that make the losers' bracket dreaded, beside the fact that all the teams in that bracket are just one game away from elimination.. It has been said that success has a hundred parents while failure is an orphan. Whoever originally coined that phrase probably thought it up while mired in the losers' bracket.

Winners bracket games are reserved for the best times in the best locations. Tournament officials everywhere intentionally reward prior wins and just as purposely punish prior losses. Losers' bracket games can, and usually are, played anywhere at anytime. When you are in the losers' bracket, you are supposed to feel grateful for any opportunity to play.

Winners' who remain in their bracket are described as "being in the catbird seat." An entire 16-team tournament can be won by winning five straight games, usually played between Friday evening and Sunday afternoon.

Losers, especially those who lose their first game early in the tournament, toil in obscurity. Each win in the losers' bracket sends some other team home and starts the wait for new blood. While five wins is sufficient to get through a weekend from the vantage point of the winners' bracket, an

The Weekend from Hell

early loser can win six games and finish the same tournament as an also-ran. This is particularly important to our story because the national tournament advancement rules in the '70s only allowed one team from each flight to reach the next qualifying level. There is no consolation prize for second place.

When Ty Stofflet was in his prime, he stood about 5'10" tall and weighed about 160 pounds. He believed in conditioning but only as it related to throwing the ball as frequently as he could and riding an indoor bike about 10 miles a day. To this day his physical form is best described as "wiry" rather than muscular.

There was nothing about him physically that would indicate an ability to stand toe to toe with bigger men and wear them down before they did the same to him. But Ty believed so much in his conditioning regimen that he said, "The other team had the best chance to score on me in the first three innings. Once the game settled down and we got into the later innings, I knew I could keep them from scoring, and the longer we stayed in extra innings the better I knew our chances were to win. I never played in an extra-inning game that I thought we could possibly lose."

If you look at pictures of the Sunners during the '70s, you will see players of every size. This is not an accident. Rocky Santilli does not allow size to interfere with his talent assessment. To paraphrase the old saying, he is far more interested in the size of the fight in the man than he is in the size of the man in the fight.

For example, Joe Lalli, the Sunners' second baseman, most likely lost an opportunity to play minor league ball because he was considered too small. Rocky described him as the best shortstop in the area and recruited him to play second base. His teammates universally considered him

Softball's Lefty Legend - Ty Stofflet

the guy who used his smarts at second to reliably get the team out of jams. Ty mentions him above all others, as the player who could think along with him and be in the right place at the right time.

And so the Sunners enter the 1970 softball season with Stofflet as their ace. The name, "Sunners," is an abbreviation for the Rising Sun Hotel, an establishment in Reading, PA, that still stands. John Kramer, its owner, was also the local sheriff. Over the years, he had forged a clear working relationship with Rocky Santilli. It is Rocky's team.

In addition to Ty, the Sunners have a pitching staff that includes Charley Booker and Clark Miller and hitters throughout the lineup. In 1970, the best hitters are Bob Yoder and Paul Price (both had minor league experience), Ty, Charley Booker and Jerry Heist. The Reading paper also frequently mentions Barry Distasio among others as a contributor to team victories.

As the season progresses, the team seems to be hitting its stride. In an Atlantic Seaboard League game, the Sunners play Flatiron of Philadelphia whose ace is George Ulmer, and defeat them in both games of a doubleheader. The double defeat is the first in Flatiron's history.

Newspaper accounts of Ty refer to him as "no-hit pitcher Ty Stofflet" for good reason. Ty is capable of throwing a no-hitter at any time. Entering the Pennsylvania State "AA" Amateur Softball Association Tournament, he is credited with three no-hitters thus far in the season. Shutouts are a regular result of his starts. The Sunners are one of the pre-tournament favorites, and are scheduled to open the tournament on Friday night in Dunmore, PA, against the defending champs, Millersville VFW.

The account of the game in the local *Reading Eagle* is

The Weekend from Hell

brief but pointed. The Rising Sun has lost the game, 3-0. Worse yet, Stofflet walked the bases loaded before giving up the winning hit. All players interviewed through the haze of 30 years suggest that one of the outfielders lost the third out of the inning in the lights, but a loss is a loss. The team needs to win seven games in a row over the next two days to advance.

Saturday in Dunmore sees the Sunners lurking in the losers' bracket. Rocky has made a secret determination. He will give his ace the ball until the Sunners go home or go on to the regional. No one else is aware of his decision nor need they be, because the Sunners must get through four games today before they can think about playing tomorrow.

In the first game against Honeybrook, the team has an easy start. The game is so one-sided (8-0) that Booker is put in relief in the fifth inning. Lalli, Ron Salvatore and Yoder hit home runs. So far, so good. Honeybrook goes home.

The second game is against Strasburg Bank of Lancaster. Lancaster gets to Ty early, scoring a run in the top of the first. The Sunners tie the game in the bottom of the second, and pull ahead for good on Ty's two-run triple in the fourth inning. Stofflet strikes out 16.

In their third game of the day, the Sunners once again draw Millersville. Stofflet shuts them out on three hits, 4-0. There is little mystery to this one as the Sunners score two runs in the top of the first inning off a hit by Price. Booker hits a home run. Millersville goes home.

The final scheduled game of the day is against Scranton. The Sunners win, 4-0, on a one-hitter by Ty. Barry Distasio has three hits in this game. According to the *Reading Eagle*, in his four games on Saturday, Ty struck out 52 and gave up one run all day.

Softball's Lefty Legend ~ Ty Stofflet

Picture a warm and pleasant Sunday morning. Three games are scheduled, the finals of the losers' bracket, the game between the finalist in the winners' and losers' brackets, and the "if" game. It is called the "if" game because it is only played if the losers' bracket winner topples the previously undefeated team. Now both teams would have a single loss, so the next game decides the tournament.

Rocky describes his morning pre-game meeting with the pitchers, catchers and coaches as follows: "So I get Ty, Clark Miller, and Charley Booker in the room along with the two catchers, the other coach and myself. I pull down the shades, lock the door and say, "How do you feel?"

Ty says, "I feel good."

I say, "Can you go three today?"

Ty says, "I don't know about that."

I say, "I keep hearing that you're better than George Ulmer, so how about if we find out? The only way I'll take you out of the game is if you tell me your arm hurts or something physically is wrong. Not that you're tired. As long as you're all right, it's not going to hurt you. Is that agreeable?"

Rocky then says, "Ty never was a very big man. People who came out to see him thought that they were going to see a big hulk. They were always surprised."

"As we're leaving the room I say, 'Unless you are physically hurt, you are throwing every game.'"

Jerry Heist, the Sunners' first-string catcher, also remembers that morning meeting. "After the meeting Rocky pulls me aside and says, 'You went four yesterday, can you go three today?' I look back at him and say, 'If he can do the pitching, I can do the catching.'"

The Sunners draw their long-time rival Allentown in the finals of the losers' bracket and win, 1-0. Yoder hits a

The Weekend from Hell

first-inning triple and scores on an error. Ty throws a two-hit shutout. The game is played in the regulation seven innings, and Allentown is sent home.

Two teams remain in the tournament, Rising Sun and South End. The winners' bracket champion has been resting in the catbird seat waiting to see who would emerge from the losers' bracket. No doubt they have fortified themselves with the knowledge that Ty has already thrown six games in less than 48 hours. South End players and fans alike were clearly hoping for another extra-inning game.

South End is the home team and draws first blood by scoring a run in the first inning. (Are you seeing a pattern?) The Sunners get one back in the fourth, four in the fifth and another in the sixth before South End scores two in the bottom of the sixth. Reading's single run in the seventh ends the scoring at 7-3, Sunners. Ty gives up six hits, according to the box score, and is in command of the game when it counts. It is now "if" game time.

The final game of the Pennsylvania State "AA" tournament lives up to its billing. South End again is home team. Nobody scores through seven innings.

In the eighth Rocky says to his coach, "I'm gonna die. If we lose this game after this talk we had in the morning and after the way he's throwing, I'll never live this down." Ty strikes out the side in the bottom of the eighth.

In the top of the ninth, Booker doubles, goes to third on a Salvatore sacrifice and is driven home by Ty. Clark Kent's alter ego does it again.

Getting back to Rocky. "So we score a run in the top of the ninth. Ty picks up his glove up, hits me with it, and says 'It's all over, Rocky.' Nine pitches later he had struck out the side."

"Ty comes running off the diamond and jumps on

Softball's Lefty Legend ~ Ty Stofflet

me," Rocky continues. "We land in a pile with him on top of me, and he's saying, 'You knew I could do it, you knew I could do it.' I'm thinking, hell if I did. All I was trying to do was get us through the tournament."

In the last game, Ty struck out 15, including the side in both the eighth and ninth innings. He threw eight games within 48 hours, winning the last one, 1-0, on his own base hit. It was one hell of a weekend in many more ways than one.

That year the Sunners were defeated in the regional and did not get to the national. The basic formula they would rely on for the next decade was established however. Count on one another and ride the big Tiger as far as he can take you.

A New Year
A Renewed Set of Hopes

IN THE BEGINNING of the 1971 season, the Sunners are maintaining an .800 winning percentage while playing most of their games against the best competition that the Atlantic Seaboard League has to offer. For example, Poughkeepsie NY, Allentown PA, South End and Strasburg Bank of Lancaster PA, and especially the Raybestos Cardinals from Stratford, CT, are all on the Seaboard schedule. Area tournaments can potentially bring in any team from anywhere on the East Coast, but generally, teams from Virginia, Maryland, New York and New Jersey find their way to Lancaster and Allentown for the Memorial Day and July 4th weekends.

In a special show of renewed hope for the future, the Sunners are building both their team roster and a new home field. The field building part is literally true. During the early months of the 1971 season a group of players, along with their manager, create a new and improved softball home field (Walt Pearson Memorial Field) with their own sweat. They used 150 tons of special softball soil to get the field in tiptop shape. According to Santilli, "We turned Pearson Field into one of the finest softball fields in the country."

It is not far-fetched to imagine Rocky working out in his mind how the best teams in the nation would be play-

Softball's Lefty Legend - Ty Stofflet

ing games hosted by the Sunners. If they were going to come, he might as well build something in which everyone associated with the Sunners could take pride.

Completion of the new field comes before the July 4th tournament in Allentown, the tournament that represents the middle of the season, and gives some idea of how well prepared a team is for the elimination tournaments that start in August. Sunners' players mentioned prominently in the hometown newspaper for their standout play are Stofflet, Price, Yoder, Lalli, Heist, Distasio and Booker.

Bob Yoder is a man of few words, but when you hit as well as he did, it's understandable. For years, he talked quite loudly with his bat. Others from the team were very happy to sing his praises for him. Yoder was a thoroughly gifted clutch hitter. Jerry Heist, the Sunners' first-string catcher in 1971, can't understand why Bob didn't become a Major League Baseball player. "Did you know," said Jerry, "that Bob once batted .398 for one of the minor league teams when he was in the Dodger organization? He could do anything he wanted to with a bat."

Ty, who benefited from Bob's hitting countless times over the years, described him as the perfect hit-and-run hitter. "Bob could use the bat like a magic wand," said Ty. "But he could also produce the long ball when the situation called for it." To be a good hit-and-run batter you need to do two things well. First, you need to figure out who will be covering either second or third base on a steal. Second, you must be able to hit the pitched ball through the hole vacated by the fielder who has left his normal position to cover the base on the steal play.

When the play is well executed, it is one of the most beautiful sights in softball. The runner on first breaks for second at the moment the ball leaves the pitcher's hand. Either

A New Year

the second baseman or shortstop moves to cover second base. If the batter hits any kind of grounder to the spot the covering infielder has just vacated, the ball rolls harmlessly into the outfield while the runner is able to continue on to third.

Jeff Seip, who softball experts consider one of the best pure hitters ever to play the game, calls Yoder the best softball hitter he ever saw. Said Seip, "You could put a can of soda out there anyplace in fair territory, and Bob could hit it." And according to Seip, "He could do it against anybody."

Ty and the Rising Sun softball club enter the July 4th Allentown tournament as the favorite. They win it in five straight games over the three-day event with Ty pitching all five. He gives up one unearned run, throws two no-hitters and is voted tournament MVP.

When asked, "When did you know that there was something different about playing with Ty?" Lalli said, "On all of the other teams that I played with, I was very superstitious. When we entered any three-day tournament, I would start out with a pair of sanitary hose (thin white socks). If we won the game on Friday night, the socks would become the lucky sanitaries. I would put them on the next day (no washing, of course.) If we won on Saturday, I would put them on again on Sunday. Once the tournament was over, I would peel them off and throw them away."

According to Lalli, "Playing with Ty, it made absolutely no difference what I wore. I could wear bloomers, I could wear nylons, I could wear anything I wanted. It didn't matter what I wore because we were going to win on Friday, we were going to win on Saturday and we were going to win on Sunday. Ty took all of my superstitions away. While I played with him I didn't have to worry about any of that."

Softball's Lefty Legend ~ Ty Stofflet

Lalli continued. "As the years went along, we used to say that we could beat anyone in the country, and later, any team in the world, 1-0, and we usually did. We even called ourselves the 'hitless wonders' but it was a misnomer. Compared to some other teams that we faced, we might not have hit that great. We didn't have to hit that great because Ty could hold anybody scoreless. We were the hitless wonders, but Ty was able to win a lot of games, 1-0. Now, in fairness, we were playing great teams with pitchers who also gave up very few runs. But give us Ty and enough time, and somehow we would figure out a way to get a run and keep them from scoring."

Here Lalli is slightly overstating the case, as in a Seaboard League game in Poughkeepsie during July, 1971, when Poughkeepsie gets four runs off Ty in the fourth inning. The Sunners come back in the bottom of the sixth to get four runs on key hits by Yoder and Price. They win the game in the 12th on a couple of hits by Lalli and Heist. That is not what "hitless wonders" do.

What seems to matter here is that the team is being molded around the idea that they can play anyone nose-to-nose and somehow trust each other to do what is necessary to win. It is clearly a one-for-all mentality. It might not be pretty, in the way that scoring a run on a passed ball to win, 1-0, is not pretty, but the Sunners will manage to get the job done.

There is something else about this team that is already beginning to stand out. Rocky has selected men who can work for the good of the team rather than worry about themselves. With Stofflet as his ace, he knows that Ty will go out of his way to communicate with everyone. No one will be snubbed or left out. Everyone will be respected.

Softball seasons can last nearly six months, with all the

A New Year

players (and many of their family members) giving up large amounts of time to devote themselves to softball. It is impossible for any player to go on summer vacations that don't involve softball and still consider himself a dedicated "AA" player. It is easy for ego and frustration to turn a long season into a team nightmare of name-calling. Cliques can sprout when players begin to resent special treatment afforded temperamental stars on the team. Ty was most happy being one of the guys. Anything that set him apart from them felt wrong to him.

Rocky didn't believe in giving anyone on the team special treatment. That philosophy was just fine with Ty. You were on the Sunners because Rocky knew that you brought something to help the team win games. If you were in the lineup, it was because Rocky believed in his heart of hearts that your talent and savvy put you there. Everyone I interviewed from the Sunners felt deeply that Rocky made decisions about playing time solely on what he thought would help the team win, not on friendship.

Ty liked being with the guys. He might be getting famous in the papers as the all-time "king" of the left-handers, but as far as his teammates are concerned, he continues to retain the common touch. A number of players mentioned how surprising it was that he was friendly with everybody. That trait was with him in Allentown at the beginning of his career and remains with him after he reaches 50 years old and is playing with youngsters. He understands how important it is to take an interest in his family, his friends and his community. The softball team at different times is all of these things wrapped together.

If you were Ty's teammate, you could count on him to do everything possible to help you feel comfortable and welcome. His behavior was both good and smart. It feels

Softball's Lefty Legend - Ty Stofflet

good to be welcomed by one of the best players of your generation. That form of acceptance can only be conveyed by attention given to the other person.

Aloofness, on the other hand, creates tension and strife. A tense or anxious player will have very poor muscle control. Physical and mental relaxation is the key to achieving optimal quickness. Players who want to generate maximum arm speed in all sports learn to keep their muscles loose. A tight grip on a bat creates a choppy swing.

If you ask Ty today what he misses most from the softball years, he will instantly tell you, "the guys." The Sunners were definitely a team that liked to enjoy themselves, and Ty could usually be found right in the middle of the fun. While any particular game might be a struggle, once it was over, win or lose, it was part of yesterday's news. It was now time to go out with the guys and have a good time. Teammates agree that he had an ever-ready sense of humor and enjoyed stopping with the guys after the game at least as much as he liked playing the game.

Today, when you visit the Stofflet family recreation room, you will find a ping-pong table, a guitar amp with a microphone, a place to throw darts and a comfortable seating area for about 10 people. You would also find, along the sidewall, a long bar with stools and a professional setup to dispense beer from a keg, should the number of guests coming into the house call for it. Friends stop in and feel welcome. The hospitality is warm and the food is Kathy's Pennsylvania Dutch home cooking

The ping-pong table was part of Ty's preparation for a new season. Pitchers, who finish their motion about 40 feet from the angry end of a metal bat, learn to value quick reflexes. Each of us at one time or another, including Ty, has been hit solidly by a batted ball, but one tries to keep

A New Year

those events to a minimum. If it were up to me, I would make it illegal to let a player go out to the mound who couldn't defend himself or herself, because I believe it is that dangerous.

Ty's solution to improve defensive reflexes for himself and his daughters who pitched was to play spirited games of ping-pong, until he and his girls could get the paddle up in time to deflect a smash. On some evenings, Ty and Kim played many games. Typical for him, he did not let her win, although he did adjust the "spot" he gave her until it became a close game. She reports not winning often but savoring every victory because she knew how much he hated to lose at ping pong or anything.

When I asked Ty's daughters to recall how they spent their summers as a softball family, they spent little time talking about Dad and his games. They were much more concerned with Mom's attempts to schedule interesting, educational trips near where the games were played.

According to her daughters, Kathy Stofflet has always believed in priorities. The children did their homework before they got to do the fun stuff. Now, when the grandchildren come over after school, Grandma Kathy will be standing around the kitchen table making sure the studies are completed. She has a smile on her face, but don't be fooled. The others know that she is smiling because she will be getting her way. The work gets done before the play begins.

Between the July 4th tournament and the Pennsylvania "AA" State Championship in August of 1971, the Sunners played a doubleheader against Green Valley Training Center of Rising Sun, MD. What makes this significant is that Herb Dudley, now 51, is the opposing pitcher. Stofflet and Dudley have only faced each other

Softball's Lefty Legend - Ty Stofflet

once, earlier that year. Dudley threw a three-hitter beating Rising Sun, 1-0.

Dudley has had one of the most illustrious pitching careers in the history of softball with the Clearwater Bombers among others. While not yet in the Hall of Fame because he hadn't retired in 1971, he is the personification of a softball legend. In this rematch between Ty Stofflet and Herb Dudley, it is Dudley who is bested, 1-0.

There is a lesson to be learned here about rating softball immortals. Not only do "the best" throw the ball harder with more stuff than other pretenders, they can also do it for more innings in a game or during a weekend or a season than anyone else. If that is not sufficient, they can play top-level ball for many years after lesser humans have gone on to much more sedentary pursuits.

What is significant in Leesport, PA, is that Herb Dudley has come to town and has left in defeat. The newspaper is proud that the local team has dethroned the king. This provides further proof that the Sunners are a force to be reckoned with. As is true of Dudley, such is the respect for Stofflet that anything done positively against him will be remembered as a source of pride no matter how old Ty is at the time.

This is a kind of gunslinger mentality that pervades most pitchers' psyches. Every game against a top competitor is a chance to gain prestige. Every win against the best proves that the contender is becoming a recognized power in his own right. Every opportunity to learn creates new ways to compete. The best thrive on the opportunities. Those who don't get to move down the pecking order of greatness.

As the state tournament approaches, the *Reading Eagle* cites Price, Barry and Gary Distasio, Yoder, Lalli, Booker,

A New Year

Jerry Heist and Bobby Heist as the Rising Sun Hotel starting lineup. Ty has seven no-hitters so far. Going into the State Championship, Ty is 7-1 in the Atlantic Seaboard League with the lone loss to Raybestos, 1-0, in eight innings.

Friday night the Sunners draw Millersville and win, 2-1. The paper notes that Stofflet has a perfect game into the seventh but gives up three straight hits to allow the run. This seems to have upset him, because the next day he pitches two no-hitters against Erie and South End to keep Reading in the winners' bracket.

Ty frequently speaks of a pitching philosophy that was alluded to separately by daughters Kim and Kris, both of whom were high school softball pitchers. (Kris also pitched in college.) "Dad's idea is simple. If someone gets a hit off you, then 'make the next one pay.'" For those of you who are thinking that hitting the next batter or some such nonsense is the way to make them pay, that was the farthest thing from his mind.

Make the next one pay means, "Get serious and strike the next batters out until the inning is over." The three hits by Millersville might have made life just a little bit more difficult for Erie and South End the next day.

On Sunday, the Sunners wait in the winners' bracket, while Millersville battles South End for the dubious honor of having to beat Ty twice to get to the regional. Jim Kauffman pitches a one-hit shutout for Millersville to beat South End, 4-0.

In the finals Stofflet faces Kauffman. The Sunners beat Millersville on a four-hit shutout. Ty strikes out 10. In the 28 innings that Stofflet has thrown in this tournament, he has struck out 53, roughly two strikeouts per inning.

Throughout his career, Ty's strikeout numbers are fairly consistent. This year against excellent "AA" Pennsylvania

Softball's Lefty Legend - Ty Stofflet

competition, Ty accounts for about two-thirds of all outs by strikeout. His teammates, therefore, have a problem that only a few fielders ever face. How do you keep alert and sharp on each pitch, knowing that there may be only one or two balls hit to you the entire game if you are in the infield? If you are in the outfield, how do you keep sharp when you might not see a ball for an entire game?

Lalli, who played second base, the most complex of the infield positions, was credited by Ty with reliably being in the right place at the right time. "Joe just seemed to have an instinct about how I was pitching and always remembered what each batter did with each pitch. If I was a little quick or slow on a pitch, he could anticipate and move a step in the right direction," said Ty. "Sometimes I would see the ball off the bat and know it was a hit. Joe would dive in the hole and we'd be out of the inning."

Joe's strategy for these games was to treat them like marathons. "Since you never know what might happen at any pitch, you have to anticipate that the ball is coming to you. Even if Ty is striking out 20 of their hitters, that 21st out could be the difference." Joe believed that he played best when he could feel the tension of the game. "I could never let up for a moment. Each play was critical," said Lalli. While there was no need to be superstitious, there was plenty of need to be quick and smart.

Considering that the Sunners are getting familiar with taking games well into extra innings against the better opponents, it is safe to assume that no one anticipates very many seven-inning games. We have hitless wonders who expect to win because they are battle tested, enjoy playing ball with one another and are able to get the most out of all their teammates. They also have Ty Stofflet. If you ask Santilli about the requirements for a great pitcher, he will

A New Year

tell you about "second gear." "The best can take over a game when they have to. The tougher the competition, the better they play."

Rocky has a championship field, a Pennsylvania "AA" State Championship, and a chance to get to the national in Springfield, MO. All he needs to do is make it out of one of the toughest regionals in the nation.

For the past 10 consecutive years, Rocky Santilli has seen Flatiron, Fox Hill or Baltimore take the regional prize and go to the ASA National. This year he knows his team is poised. But there is the old saying: the games have to be played on the field and the better team does not always win.

The 1971 Central Atlantic Regional "AA" Softball Tournament is played on Guy Mason Field in Washington, D.C. Once again, it is loaded with high caliber competition. The Rising Sun team from Reading finds itself in the toughest bracket, needing to beat Fox Hill, Flatiron, and Green Valley Training Center in its first three games to make it to the winners' bracket championship game.

The Friday night tournament opener turns out to be a typical Sunners tournament "rout," that is, another nail biter. The score remains 0-0 through 11 innings. In the top of the 12th, Yoder hits a home run off Ron Peterson and Price hits a double, eventually scoring on some sloppy fielding by Fox Hill. Stofflet pitches a three-hit shutout and records 20 strikeouts in 12 innings. The final score is 2-0, Sunners.

Their next opponent on Saturday is Flatiron AC of Philadelphia with George Ulmer on the mound. The tournament schedule has Flatiron meeting the winner of the Rising Sun – Fox Hill Game. This will be Flatiron's first game and Rising Sun's second. George Ulmer will be thor-

Softball's Lefty Legend - Ty Stofflet

oughly rested. Many of you might know from baseball or softball experience, however, that dropball pitchers do best when their arm is a bit tired. George Ulmer has one of the best dropballs in the country.

Whereas a riseball pitcher when rested can get something more on the pitch to help it defy gravity, an intended dropball thrown too fast may stay flat. Anything that stays flat to these hitters might as well be post-marked, because it's going to be sent on a journey.

Reading gets an improbable 10 hits off Ulmer and routs Flatiron, 5-0. Ty fans 13 in seven innings and allows two sixth-inning singles. He is striking out batters at his usual rate of two Ks (strikeouts) per inning.

If there is a plan to bump the Sunners into the losers' bracket by making them play the best competition right off, that strategy has failed. After a 2:30 p.m. Saturday game, the Sunners are done for the day. Families can sit around the pool or see the Washington D.C., sites. Dinner can occur at a reasonable time. It is the softball equivalent of a life of leisure.

It is left to Fox Hill and Flatiron to play into the night, beating lesser teams for the honor of getting to the championship game. As noted earlier in reference to the 1970 Pennsylvania State Tournament, there are a number of problems, both physical and mental, that make early-tournament losers extremely unlikely to win the tournament. The starting times for the losers' games can often be backed up by either bad weather or extra-inning contests. And all the teams know that Ty and the Sunners are sitting pretty with plenty of rest and relaxation.

Although this tournament is scheduled over four days, the winner of the losers' bracket has to win a doubleheader from the winners' bracket champ in order to win the

A New Year

tournament. Because all tournaments are scheduled this way beforehand, it is fair, but looking up from the depths of the losers' bracket, it seems anything but fair.

On Sunday, against Green Valley, Lalli hits a second-inning home run. In the third, Price, Art Weida and Stofflet hit consecutive singles, making the score 2-0. In all, the Sunners get eight hits and Ty scatters four.

The winners' bracket final is scheduled for Sunday night. Their opponent is Brothers Furniture of Washington, D.C., the tournament host. In the fourth inning, the Sunners play good old-fashioned softball. Heist walks, steals second and comes in to score the only run of the game on a single by Barry Distasio. This sends Brothers Furniture back to the finals of the losers' bracket where they lose to Fox Hill.

The championship game against Fox Hill on Monday is settled early. In the bottom of the first inning, Bobby Heist hits a two-run single and that is the extent of the scoring. Ty is the Most Valuable Pitcher and Yoder is selected the Most Valuable Hitter of the tournament. Looking back over the tournament, the Sunners clearly gained momentum with each game. True, they needed 12 innings to get past Fox Hill, but if you remember Lalli's thinking, a 0-0 game means "we got them all the way."

Rocky has done it. He has put together a team that earned its way to the national. No break in the drawings, no easy games on the schedule. His best hitter is acknowledged for his great tournament and his ace has the sort of reputation that brings trepidation to the other team before they see him play.

Ty has pitched five shutouts, including 40 consecutive shutout innings. Pitchers are typically rated by Earned Run Average (ERA), which means that runs scored against the team by errors of some sort are not counted against the ERA. Ty has not allowed a run of any kind, tainted or otherwise. The oldest ballplaying axiom is "THEY CAN'T WIN IF THEY DON'T SCORE." Stofflet has made it impossible for the other team to win. There is nothing more that a pitcher can do to keep the team in the game.

During these early national champion years, the Sunners are a team "on a shoestring." Everything is done as inexpensively as possible. Remember, earlier that year, the home field in Leesport, PA, was assembled literally by the team. Now it is time to get to Springfield, MO, and everyone will be taking their own automobiles and meeting at the motel.

The 1971 ASA National Fast Pitch Softball Championship is played in Springfield, MO, September 10-17. It is an eight-day tournament drawing 20 teams from around the country, including a representative from the Armed Forces. The Sunners have drawn a first-round bye and will play the winner of the match up between Clearwater, FL, and the Armed Forces team. The Armed Forces wins, 4-1, on the first day and plays the Sunners on the second.

This is the Sunners' and Ty's first time in the ASA National. While Ty has already won an International Softball Congress world title with Sal's Lunch in 1969, the ASA has a more highly regarded consistent level of competition throughout its 20-team roster. Since Ty is playing in the "show me" state of Missouri, it's time for him to show what he can do on this expanded national stage. And show them is what he is about to do.

He comes into this tournament with nine no-hitters to his credit, and he has gone through the Central Atlantic Regional Tournament without giving up a run of any kind.

A New Year

However, as far as the good people from Missouri are concerned, he is just another upstart who will be getting a dose of the best-of-the-best. After he is tested, his worth can be determined. One has the idea that it was also the way Ty was thinking.

In the second inning against the Armed Forces, Stofflet singles and takes third on an outfield error. He scores the first Sunner run on a passed ball. Lalli's single in the same inning gets misplayed into a run-scoring error. That score holds until the top of the sixth when the Sunners score two more runs. Ty hits a triple to score Weida and is plated by Bob Heist.

In the bottom of the sixth the opposing pitcher, Godlin, ends Ty's shutout pitching streak of 45 consecutive innings with a home run. The next inning the Sunners score four runs off a reliever. The Armed Forces finishes with a single run in the seventh. The Rising Sun stays in the winners' bracket with an auspicious beginning (8-2). Fort Worth is their next opponent.

Fort Worth comes into the tournament with a 101-4 record and is the favorite in this game. Apparently, Ty does not read other teams' press clippings because when the dust has settled, he has pitched a perfect game. In a perfect game nobody reaches first base safely for any reason. A pitcher can face 21 batters in a seven- inning game, but if one of them reaches first base and is picked off or erased in a double play, etc., it is not a perfect game.

Here is the perfect combination of pitcher and team. The catcher must hold all third strikes and the fielders must be flawless. A perfect game is just what the label states – perfect. The Sunners win this game, 7-0, but it was 1-0 through the top of the sixth. They play a bit of fast pitch, little-ball strategy again in the sixth until Yoder caps

Softball's Lefty Legend ~ Ty Stofflet

matters with a three-run home run. Ty starts the sixth-inning rally with a single.

Nothing sets a tournament to talking like a perfect game. This Pennsylvania Dutchman and his mates have humbled Fort Worth and its 101-4 record. Who is this guy?

There is a story by Anvil Welch in the *Springfield Times* during the tournament that captures the mood of the Springfield fans. Welch notes that Stofflet has rapidly become a household name to the locals. Next they face Cedar Rapids, IA.

The opposing pitcher is Richie Stephen, who deserves recognition because he is locked into a 0-0 game after 14 innings. While Ty winds up striking out 33. Stephen seems to get out of one jam after another. However, a play at home in the fifth inning, when Barry Distasio is called out on a wild pitch, permanently taints this game for all who were there. All players interviewed get that special "we got robbed" looked when they talk about that play.

Thirty-three years later, no other play raises the hackles at the back of their necks more than that call. The consensus was that it wasn't even close enough to be in doubt. But judgment calls are not open to appeal and the game moves along.

In the 15th inning, Cedar Rapids scores two runs without getting the ball into the outfield. An infield hit, a walk and a seeing-eye blooper just beyond second base scores the deciding run. A second run scores on a ball past the catcher, Heist. Even in defeat, Ty is continuing to generate big waves in the deep waters of the national. In three games he has been brilliant, and his team has proved very tough against top competition.

The Sunners next face Oklahoma City and win, 3-1. It is an important game because they have to make a comeback to prevail. They are now without their sure-handed

A New Year

shortstop, Gary Distasio, who is hospitalized with a viral infection. A hospital is the last place anyone wants to be, particularly hundreds of miles from home. But hospitals are a part of softball play. Just pick out the tournament hosts and they will be sure to know the location of the nearest good hospital.

The Sunners are now being described as the Cinderella team in the tournament, but they must face the defending national champion Raybestos Cardinals, and the Cardinals are not known for any sentimentality. A couple of hits and a couple of errors put three runs on the board in the Cardinal third.

For all intents and purposes that is the inning that ends the tournament for Reading. The final score is 5-3, with Ty taken out of the game in the sixth to a standing ovation by 7,000 fans. The people of the "Show Me" state have been shown a lot, and they appreciate the effort.

At the end of the tournament, ultimately won by Cedar Rapids over Raybestos, an all-star team is selected. Ty is voted Most Valuable Player in the tournament for a 3-2 pitching record combined with a .375 batting average. Roy Burlison is voted Most Valuable Pitcher. Paul Price, Sunner center fielder, is selected to the second all-star team.

When asked about his ace, Rocky makes a very good show of softball diplomacy. He will state publicly that Ty is a good pitcher but he is not ready to bestow any superlatives just yet. Rocky will admit that Ty is the best fielding pitcher he has ever seen and he is calling Ty possibly the best lefty in the game, but this is not the time for any statements that might come back to haunt him when they return to the national.

Rocky Santilli has taken his team to the national, played the ultimate winner to a standstill, and, in his

Softball's Lefty Legend - Ty Stofflet

mind, won the game that sent the Sunners into the losers' bracket. He comes away from the tournament knowing that he has one of the best pitchers in the country, in his prime (Ty is 30 years old in 1971). Some teammates are getting up around 40, but the team now believes that they can compete against anyone with their ace. Rocky knows that the Pennsylvania Hills seem to grow exceptional players with regularity. He will continue to scour the area for top talent.

Ty is now a household name in both the ISC and the ASA. Wherever he goes, he has a knack of behaving in a way that brings new MVP trophies to his trophy case, and loyal fans to his entourage. Just this year, he has been MVP in the state championship, the regional championship and the national championship. Some trifecta indeed.

Ty's Growing Fan Base

THE WORD ABOUT TY has been spreading ever since he began pitching in Allentown in 1960. No matter how menacing or ferocious he looks from the mound, he does not carry himself as a threat anywhere outside the lines of play. The Kevin Costner movie, *Field of Dreams*, includes a scene in which one of the dream team ballplayers, played by Burt Lancaster, must go beyond the magic field to the stands to keep a little girl from choking. He makes the choice and is immediately transformed from a ballplayer to something else (in this case, a doctor). Ty had the ability in real life to transform himself the moment the game began and the moment the game was over.

Everyone interviewed who played with or against Ty reported that he could make the transformation from mild mannered, pre-game warmup to game-time intensity in the time it took to walk out to the mound from the bench. He was called tough but not mean and from the perspectives of fans watching his performances, he was a combination of blazing speed and precise movement through space.

Certainly, one of the things going for him was that at 5'10" and 160 pounds he looked middle-sized. Most of his opponents were larger. He had a catlike agility and grace. In fact, the words that anyone has used to describe his fielding were consistently related to feline attributes, either

Softball's Lefty Legend - Ty Stofflet

cat or tiger. He is an average-sized person who had a very non-average ability to get the job done anywhere on a softball field.

While I believe that his size certainly contributed to his growing fan base, it is his personality that connected them to him. And that personality has at its core the idea that performing for people can be a whole lot of fun.

Did you know that for a little more than a decade, Ty was the lead singer in a country and western band named the Koachmen? The group began when he was about 17 and played in late-night clubs in and around Easton, PA. Ty is quite musical, although he is not a formally trained musician. His guitar playing was a source of joy for many years. The band was successful in booking music jobs on weekends, and you know that the people in the audience were having fun along with the band.

When Ty talks about his band years, he might as well be talking about a softball team. The guys had to get along so they could do their best on stage. It was okay to question each other before you got on the bandstand, but once in front of the audience with an open mike, it had to be harmony, harmony, harmony. Chords for tunes had to be worked out in advance as well as the individual arrangements for each piece of music. No player could freelance or the group wouldn't sound musical.

In addition, good bands learn to get in tune with their audience. Over time they become sensitive, friendly and responsive to the likes and dislikes of the crowd. But mainly, they have a knack for pleasing the people who have come to hear them perform. Maybe they will come back.

Don Van Deusen, a shortstop-second baseman who joined the team in 1980, described an event that illustrates the point. By the time Van Deusen joined the team, Ty was

Ty's Growing Fan Base

a major drawing card for all of fast pitch softball. He had been featured in *Sports Illustrated*, and had become used to playing for thousands of visiting fans whenever the team traveled.

According to Van Deusen, Ty had pitched the opener of an exhibition series against the All-American Bar team in Minnesota sometime in the early '80s. By this time he is over 40 years old and has suffered a career-threatening wrist break that prevented him from playing the entire 1980 season. According to Van Deusen, "He lost an 11-inning game, 1-0, so you know that he was worn out. After the game, what usually happened was that a lot of people, the media, and softball enthusiasts would wait until he came out and would just talk to him. He handled that so well."

Van Deusen added, "This was after losing a tough game. He had pitched his heart out and we couldn't get him a run. He was always patient and kind. I can remember other softball pitchers coming up to him and asking how he threw his changeup. He was always very kind."

Don remembers it to this day as an extraordinary act of caring. Neither of us could imagine many others doing such a thing. Ty did it with regularity.

Starting All Over Again

IN THE 1972 SEASON, the Sunners are described as the Atlantic Seaboard champs, the State champs, the Eastern Central regional champs and the fourth-place finishers of the ASA "AA" national tournament. Their 52-10 record in 1971 is well publicized along with the fact that Larry Bergh, from Allentown, PA, will be their No. 2 pitcher. The team has also added Art Weida, whom they had picked up for some tournament games the year before, and Paul Troika from Reading.

Larry Bergh has an interesting story. At 6'8" he looks every bit the ABA basketball player he was, even though he started playing basketball relatively late. He moved to Allentown and began throwing while he was catching for a friend. It is the same story that the Hall of Fame pitcher, Jimmy Moore, tells about himself. Neither Larry nor Jimmy thought very much about being a pitcher until each found that he could learn to throw a softball quickly, using the underhand motion without much strain.

Very big men can be devastating dropball pitchers. Their height and the location of the ball when it leaves their hand combines to create a pitch that "falls off a table." You and everyone else in the stadium may know that the pitch is coming. Hitting it anywhere except into the ground is a problem that few hitters ever solve consis-

Softball's Lefty Legend - Ty Stofflet

tently. Dropball pitching puts a premium on solid infield play, and it makes a catcher's life miserable, but the Sunners are demonstrating that they can make the plays in all sorts of pressure situations.

Bergh is also a tough guy between the lines and a pleasant one outside of them. He has locked horns with Ty often in the Allentown weekday league and enjoys the challenge. "In those games we could always expect to go more than seven innings." He respects and likes Ty, and he also is aware that Ty is better than any other pitcher he has encountered. He is there to be the second pitcher and will do his best in that role.

If you ask Rocky what the key to team harmony is, he will mention respect for each player's ability to contribute. But then he will point out that the players who are not starting must be aware of why the other players have been placed ahead of them. False pride is just as big a problem as false modesty. Santilli made it a practice to get playing time for everybody, particularly on four-game, Atlantic Coast League weekends. He needed everybody to be ready to step in, but he required that they understand the thinking behind the hierarchy or they could foment trouble.

In 1972 Rocky is sticking to the game plan. He is selecting his players from a tight geographic area, which helps build a close-knit feeling from people who understand each other. In the national he played against teams that were comprised of players brought together from a number of states.

Stories abound of particular players in the nationals who happened to have magnificent tournament performances. At the end of the tournament, a team owner who also happens to own a company may offer a player from another team a job opportunity. The deal is struck and the

Starting All Over Again

player moves to his new team. Sometimes it turns out to be a match made in heaven; other times, not so heavenly.

Rocky does not have that option, so he is forced to keep his team completely home grown. In many other parts of the country, that might have proved a handicap. In the lushness of his valleys, players seem to be growing everywhere.

The Sunners are clearly a team on the rise (sorry about the pun). Ty is throwing shutouts, no-hitters and perfect games once again, and tournament opponents seem to be vying for second place. In the July 4th, 1972 Allentown tournament, Ty pitches all five games. Scores are no longer 0-0 going into extra innings. The team is winning by much bigger margins. For example, the Allentown tournament Rising Sun games were 8-0, 3-0, 1-0, 5-0 and 8-1. In the 1-0 game, the team scored in the third inning. The 8-0 victory included a perfect game performance.

In league and exhibition games, Ty and Larry are splitting assignments. It is part of Rocky's plan. "Whenever I could, I tried to keep Ty from being overused. Larry Bergh was a great pitcher who could have been the No. 1 on many teams. He deserved to pitch for us as often as he did."

To this day Ty and Larry are good friends who often bowl together. Even in the world of bowling competition, Ty is a perfectionist. Within the past two seasons, he has bowled two perfect games. He can describe the precision required to put a bowling ball in the pocket with the same intensity he uses to speak about softball pitching. It's just part of the way the man is built.

One of the obvious bonds between Stofflet and Bergh is that each respects the other's talent. Larry mentions his amazement at Ty's softball memory. "Anytime I would ask

Softball's Lefty Legend - Ty Stofflet

Ty about a batter I had faced who gave me trouble, he would remember the hitter and his swing. He would then tell me how to pitch to that guy. When I did what he said, it worked."

Ty and the other players who played with Bergh during his 10 years with the Sunners remember Bergh's uncanny ability to pick up an opposing pitcher's pitch before it left his pitcher's hand.

Joe Lalli, who, in addition to his sparkling play for the Sunners, is a member of George Washington University's Sports Hall of Fame, recalls pitch stealing in the Atlantic Seaboard League.

"Our pitcher, Larry Bergh, could call the other pitcher's pitches if he was on the side of the pitcher's throwing arm. I remember going to Poughkeepsie and being in a game when he could call the pitches. Not everybody wanted to know. I wanted to know because my problem was that I couldn't lay off the riser. When Larry signaled a riser, I could take it.

"That works perfectly on Friday night. On Saturday, Larry calls the riser, and this guy throws a fastball right down the middle and strikes me out. I'm just standing there with the bat on my shoulders. I knew our goose was cooked. From that moment we went back to playing regular softball again."

As defending champion, Rising Sun has a slot in the 1972 Central Atlantic Regional Tournament. It is an 11-team tournament and the Reading team has drawn Millersville. In a nine-inning contest, they lose to Kauffman, 2-1. This puts it in the losers' bracket and it will take five straight wins to get to the national.

Dave Pyle Pontiac of Marlow Heights, MD, is defeated (6-0) on a one-hitter. Paul Troika, new to the team this

Starting All Over Again

year, hits a home run in that game. The Sunners then beat Flatiron (3-1) and Millersville (3-0) to finish Sunday's schedule.

In the finals of the losers' bracket, played just before the championship game, the Sunners do the one thing that a losers' bracket team can ill afford to do. They get caught up in a 12-inning game against Danville, VA. They win, 3-1, but they have dug a deep hole.

In the meantime, the Shaeffer team from Baltimore has been waiting in the winners' bracket, watching the extra-inning game. They know that Ty will have to pitch another 14 innings in order to win the tournament.

The Sunners win the first game, 2-1. Yoder hits a home run and scores the second run on a hit by Weida. In the "if" game, Baltimore scores three runs in the first and one in the third. John Erney finishes the game for Ty as the Rising Sun Hotel loses, 5-1.

That year, the program cover for the national, played in Dallas, Texas, featured a game-shot photo of Ty in his red Rising Sun uniform. The party was ready to receive the previous year's Cinderella team and its MVP pitcher. But for the 10th time in 11 years, the Sunners don't make it out of the regionals. The Brooklyn Dodgers are not the only team that had use for the phrase, "Wait 'til next year."

The Team Refuses to Stand Still

ROCKY SANTILLI IS A BUILDER. One can imagine that shortly after the 1972 season he was already designing the next additions to his Sunner team. One new name in particular is important in this year's rendition of the Sunners, Carl Solarek. By this time Gerry Heist is 40. He has been the workhorse for the team's catching corps, but as all of us learn, time waits for no man. The years behind the plate have done their damage to his knees. No matter how much Rocky values his catcher, he must prepare the team for replacements, particularly in key positions.

Carl Solarek brings with him an expertise behind the plate forged by a five-year stint in the Detroit Tigers organization. His tale is a common one among the former Minor League ball players interviewed for this book. He went into the minors after high school and was completely trained anew as to how to play his position, how to hit, and how to think about baseball in general. According to him, they even decided which catcher's mitt was acceptable to use.

Solarek will have time to break into this "AA" fast pitch game, but fairly quickly he and Ty develop a rapport that will last 10 years as battery mates. This year Gerry will do most of the catching and Carl will be able to get a sense of the flow of these kinds of games. Over time he will become ready for the transition.

This brings up a point about Ty and his catchers. Five catchers who played with Ty are united in this perception: Ty was a communicator who wanted his catcher to be a source of help and partnership during a game. There are pitchers who are quite fussy about whom they allow in the pitcher's circle. Ty would gladly accept any source of help, particularly if a pitch wasn't working.

If he got a tip that he could use immediately (like the stride is too long or the glove is not going far enough behind the back before the release), Ty was the kind of pitcher to try out the suggested solution on the next pitch. If it worked, he would point right back at the catcher with a salute.

Another thing that each of those catchers mentioned is Ty's use of the changeup. He would never throw a change-up if the drop was called, but if he was supposed to throw the riseball he might throw the changeup on his own. On his own means that he would nod agreement with the catcher's signal for a rise and then somewhere in mid-pitch he would change his mind.

Ty was able to do this because he would take the catcher's signal with the ball in his glove hand. As his hands came up over his head to a position behind his head, he would put his left hand into the glove and grip the ball. It was such a blur of motion that the other team could not pick up just what he was going to throw. And if it seemed like the opponent could tell what pitch was coming from something that the catcher did, Ty could always change his mind in mid-pitch. Tom Wagner, the manager of Pay 'n Pak and other Seattle-based teams, called Ty the toughest

The Team Refuses to Stand Still

pitcher to read.

The Rising Sun wins its first 11 games, but suffers a double defeat to Raybestos. Ty loses the first Raybestos game, 2-1, in 13 innings. The July 4th tournament in Allentown is a three-weekend affair. The Sunners win their part of the tournament and wait two weeks to meet the winner of the second flight. In front of about 3,000 fans in Allentown, the Sunners beat Frank's Collision of Philadelphia, with Ty and Larry pitching parts of the two games. The scores are 9-3 and 4-1. Later that month, Ty and Larry beat the Long Island Merchants with two no-hitters. By this time the Sunners are 27-4.

Towards the end of July, 1973, the Sunners take their first off the continent trip when they visit the Bermuda National Team. The team plays nine exhibition games in Bermuda and wins them all. Most are blowouts. Stofflet, Bergh and Booker each win games on this trip. Ty adds two more no-hitters, consecutively: against Bermuda International, he pitches a perfect game and strikes out the last 15, then he strikes out the first 13 in the next game for 28 strikeouts in a row.

Back in the U.S., the Sunners again face Raybestos and lose a doubleheader, 7-6 and 5-0. One gets the idea that even the Sunners do not play well having to bear down after having such a glorious vacation in Bermuda. But they get back to their game the next week against Poughkeepsie with a doubleheader sweep. Ty wins the first game, 1-0, in 10 innings. He then relieves Larry Bergh in the third inning of the second game and wins, 3-2, in eight. Rocky is setting up his rotation for the upcoming qualifying tournaments. Ty needs to be ready to pitch at any time.

The Sunners enter the Pennsylvania "AA"

Softball's Lefty Legend - Ty Stofflet

Championship Tournament, held at their own Walt Pearson Field, as the clear favorites. They possess a gaudy record against Seaboard competition. Only Raybestos, which qualifies from its home state of Connecticut, has been able to solve the problem of how to beat them consistently.

The state championship goes according to form. The Sunners win it in four straight. Ty wins three and Larry one. In the first game, another "hitless wonders" laugher, 1-0, Ty gets by Millersville, which once again has Kauffman on the mound. Gerry Heist drives in Rennie Petre with the only tally. In the tournament finale, Ty strokes an RBI single in the sixth to tie the game, again against Millersville. In the eighth, the Sunners get two more and head to the regional in Winchester, VA.

Between the state and the regional, the Sunners had a four-game set against Raybestos in Leesport. The Sunners are able to score only once in the four games and lose three times to drop their Seaboard record to 23-9. In their lone victory, Ty pitched a shutout and scored the only run on a triple by Paul Troika. The four scores were 1-0, 1-0, 1-0 and 3-0. In the 3-0 game, Booker pitched for the Sunners.

In the regional, the Sunners start with a 9-1 rout of the D.C. Raiders. In the second game, with Ty pitching in 100-degree heat, the Sunners win, 9-0. Ty hits a home run and gets relieved in the fifth.

In the third game, Ty and Rising Sun beat Godfrey V. W., 1-0. Ty loses the no-hitter with two outs in the seventh, but the win moves the Sunners to the finals of the winners' bracket where they beat Fox Hill, 3-0. Up until this moment, all of the cliches apply. The Sunners are winning easily or winning by being tough, but they are cruising toward another date with national competition. As of

The Team Refuses to Stand Still

Sunday, September 2, they are set to play either Flatiron or Fox Hill on Monday, whoever survives from the losers' bracket.

Fox Hill opens the day by beating Flatiron. The finals follow immediately. Within three hours, Fox Hill has beaten Ty and the Sunners, 2-1 and 2-0. Ty has struck out only six in each game. Fox Hill manages nine hits in the first game and six hits in the second. It is, by all accounts, a stunning performance.

This is clearly one of the low points in the history of the Sunners. After being the Cinderella darlings of the Springfield tournament, the Sunners have failed to survive the rigors of the regionals for these next two years. And there is nothing particularly new or different about the outcome of these last two games, except that the other team outhits and outscores the team from Leesport, PA, in both.

That makes 12 times in 13 years that the Sunners have failed to reach the nationals, three out of four with Ty as their ace. This would be a sad story were it not for the character, talent and dedication of the men who played for the Sunners. Their ace got beat by a team that had a day that was hotter than the weather. Time to lick one's wounds, grab a couple of cold ones, and head back home.

When Life Presents Obstacles...

IT IS EASY FOR A TEAM to stay together when it is successful, and in many ways the Sunners are successful. But in the way that matters most to Rocky and Ty, in three of the past four years, somebody else has carried home the brass ring. Rocky's reaction is quite telling. "In the years that we lost to Fox Hill, Flatiron or Baltimore, none of those teams did very well in the nationals."

You can almost hear him mutter under his breath, "Why did you do so well in the regionals if you weren't going to tear it up in the nationals?" But the games are won and lost on the field and when your two losses eliminate you, it's time to smile and start the wait.

Rocky has a plan this year. Although most players are returning to old positions, he feels the need to become younger at catcher. It is all part of the oldest rule of softball – "strength and speed up the middle" provide the best defense. In the case of Solarek, the apprenticeship is over. It is time for the five-year pro to start pushing his weight around.

The batteries now read Stofflet-Solarek, Bergh-Heist, and once again the Rising Sun team from Reading, PA, overmatches nearly everyone it faces. Bill McNelis is the third pitcher in the rotation, having transferred from Poughkeepsie.

By the 1974 Men's "AA" Softball Central Atlantic

Softball's Lefty Legend ~ Ty Stofflet

Regional at Conlin Field, Lancaster, PA, Ty is 25-3 with 381 strikeouts in 203 innings. The leading hitters are Price (.364), Solarek (.309), Troika (.290) and Distasio (.284).

Stofflet wins the opening game, 5-1, with 18 strikeouts and no walks. McNelis wins the second game, 6-2, against George Ulmer and Collex, and McNelis wins the third, 3-0, against Portsmouth, VA. Ty wins the fourth against Carling, 4-0, and the finale against the Fox Hill team, now called F & M Bankers of Hampton, VA. In this return match against the team that beat him twice on the same day in the prior year's tournament, Stofflet strikes out 12 and does not allow a hit until the seventh with two out. Rising Sun wins, 2-0.

For his efforts, Ty is named the Most Valuable Pitcher. F & M Bankers can go home; the Sunners will be on their way to Clearwater, FL, for the national. This is a classic Stofflet performance. Remember the defeat and let it sting – then make them pay.

To play in Clearwater, the Pennsylvania ball club sets out by car in order to arrive at the tournament for a Saturday game. Their first game starts at 8:00 a.m. and Rocky blames himself for not having his team ready. "We drove most of Friday and got in late Friday night. For a tournament of this importance, we should have been there with a day to spare."

What Rocky is describing is something I call a "learning loss." In a learning loss, something unexpected happens for which the person experiencing the loss is not as prepared as someone who has been in that same situation before. Think of it as rookie mistakes. You have to get your feet wet under this brand of tournament competition in order to learn how to make the most of your opportunities in the future.

When Life Presents Obstacles...

Rocky believes that his team was "flat" Saturday morning. However, this was the grand stage, and Ty had already felt the heady feeling of being the most valuable player in the 1971 tournament. They draw the Carson, CA, team and play to a standstill for 14 innings. Ty throws a one-hitter for those 14 innings, striking out 21.

The top of the 15th inning is best described by Rocky. "In a lot of ways, Ty was like a high spirited race horse. He did everything fast. He threw fast, he fielded his position fast, and he ran fast. As the leadoff batter in the top of the 15th inning, Ty stretches a double into a triple by using his speed. He slides head first into third base and the third baseman steps on his pitching hand. His hand is bleeding, but he stays in the game. We don't score him in three tries, and he goes back out to the mound. On the first pitch of the bottom of the inning, his hand is bleeding so badly that he gets blood on the ball and has to be taken out of the game."

McNelis relieves and the other team immediately scores to win. Stofflet gets credit for a no-decision and 14 innings of shutout ball. The Sunners are temporarily without their ace but this year they have come prepared. They will need to win nine games. Everybody will get a chance to contribute.

Bergh beats Las Vegas, 9-2, and the next day McNelis beats Rogersville, TN, 5-2. The team is rallying and the bats have come to life. Ty has also had some time to heal. He is mending his wounds and, for the time being, the big show seems to be getting along without him. It is time for him to return to action.

The opponent is from Detroit and happens to be the team that is about to pay for what happened in the Sunners' first game. Nothing personal, but it is the Stofflet

Softball's Lefty Legend ~ Ty Stofflet

way to make somebody pay. When the last out is recorded, the score is 1-0, Sunners, and Ty has pitched another no-hitter in the nationals. The ace is back where he belongs, and once a day some other team is sent home by the Rising Sun.

The next opponent is Mankato, MN, and Ty pitches another shutout, 2-0, aided by singles in the sixth and seventh inning. The next game is against Carson, CA. McNelis gets the start and the win. Ty enters in the sixth, preserving the shutout, and has now thrown 29 1/3 consecutive scoreless innings.

In the next game, Gaslight of Springfield, MO, scores three unearned runs to beat Rising Sun, 3-0. Ty is credited with 35 1/3 consecutive innings without allowing an earned run, but if you remember the earlier description about earned and unearned runs, both types can lead to a pitching loss. Ty loses on throwing errors, giving up one hit in the final game. But he says it best, "We win as a team, and we lose as a team."

For the second time in as many tries in the nationals, the Rising Sun Hotel has come in fourth, and its pitching star has grabbed the limelight with a stellar and gutsy performance. After being injured on the pitching hand, Ty comes back and garners the coveted Most Valuable Player Award.

For those of you who might be confused, the Most Valuable Player Award is a one-of-a-kind honor for each tournament. It automatically puts the player on the All-America team for that year, and it sets that player apart from all others for particularly outstanding play. In two national appearances, Ty has taken home both MVP trophies.

If you have had or get an opportunity to talk to Ty,

When Life Presents Obstacles...

however, you will learn quickly that individual trophies in a team sport have a hollow ring if the team doesn't also capture the gold. Nowhere is it written, "Rising Sun Hotel, National Champions." There's still plenty of work to do.

Bringing It Home

THE SUNNERS START THE 1975 season with a number of open wounds. In 1974, Carl Solarek, his first year at the national, is responsible for two wild throws that lead to the three runs scored in the Sunners' final tournament loss. It is quite safe to bet that he is itching to have a second opportunity on the national stage. Solarek is a softspoken fellow, as are many who have already proved their toughness beyond further testing. He has had five years as a catcher in the Tigers organization. He considers himself a professional ballplayer and the last game does not sit right.

Stofflet has once again proved to everyone's satisfaction that he possesses personal talents that demand individual recognition. But he does not play the game for individual recognition. He plays for team championships. For the second time, his team has gone home before the tournament has concluded. There is no way he can tolerate that outcome.

But the person who feels most disturbed and most responsible for the 1974 fourth-place finish in the national is Rocky Santilli. In his own words, "Now all winter I'm disturbed. I said at all the team meetings, 'Fellows, I don't know how we're going to get there. The tournament is in California. There's no way we can drive. This year, we're going to fly. We're going to go there Thursday night,

Softball's Lefty Legend - Ty Stofflet

because if we get a game Friday night, we want to be prepared to play.'"

He goes on, "We're going to treat this tournament like everybody else treats it. We have the team to win, so we're going to win. All summer I'm like a broken record – 'we're going to win, we're going to win, we're going to win.'"

But getting the players excited was not his only goal. It was time to alert the community to the impending success that the Sunners will be having in Hayward, CA, as well. "And beyond that, I used to go into the *Reading Eagle* newspaper every Wednesday night. I would tell the guys that we're going to win the national. And this year, the team that wins the national represents the United States in the World Games in New Zealand. As true as I sit here, when I was leaving the sports department, the newsmen would laugh."

"I found out much later that when I left the paper to go home, they used to say, 'He's a kook, he doesn't have a clue about what's going on.' Every Wednesday, though, I'd give them the weekend schedule."

Rocky had another problem. He had promised the team that he would find a way to get them to Hayward. This was a team on a shoestring though, and getting the money would require some quick thinking and even quicker talking. Here's how he did it. "I knew a guy who owned a travel agency and I called him and said, 'Hey, I've got a problem. My team is too good to have to drive to California. We can't afford to pay you now, but somehow when we get back from the national tournament, we'll get you paid.' The guy agreed. I wrote a note and we got the tickets."

In 1975, it is clear that everything leading up to the Central Atlantic Regional Major Softball League

Bringing It Home

Championship at Hopewell, VA, might as well be considered pre-season. Just for the record, however, the Sunners win the Allentown Patriots July 4th Tournament every year between 1970-1978.

The five games in the 1975 regional are anything but a cakewalk. The Sunners open with Stofflet's 13-strikeout, no-hit 1-0 victory against Bucky's of Baltimore. Hitless wonders softball. The Sunners' next three games are more comfortable, with Stofflet and Bergh sharing the load, but the final is a good old-fashioned nail-biter.

In the championship game against F & M Bankers of Norfolk, VA, Ty strikes out 33 in a 19-inning, 2-1 win. The victory earns them a plane trip to the destination envisioned by their manager since the last minute of the last game in Clearwater, FL. Ty has appeared in all five regional games and is credited with 80 strikeouts.

The Sunners draw Poughkeepsie in the opening game of the national, which was guaranteed to make them happy and Poughkeepsie upset. For the past few years, the Sunners have improved to the point where Poughkeepsie is a good warmup. The team gets seven runs on 11 hits. Ty throws a 13 strikeout, two-hit shutout. A great way to open on Friday night. One thing is certain – Santilli is feeling good about his decision to make sure that everybody arrived on Thursday.

Saturday night's opponent, Detroit, is much tougher, but the outcome is the same. The Sunners win, 1-0, on a one-hit, 11-strikeout performance by Stofflet. The Sunners also get only one hit, but it is a home run by Gary Distasio in the seventh inning. They seem to be showing the right amount of toughness, turning a one-hit performance into a victory.

It is the third game that fans and players alike remem-

Softball's Lefty Legend ~ Ty Stofflet

ber, because it is against Pay 'n Pak, the highly-regarded team from Seattle. This game has a moment that Ty remembers because it shows the growing respect and rapport that he and Solarek have achieved in their three years together.

As Ty tells it, "Pay 'n Pak was a tough team who could hit, there's no doubt about that." In the fifth inning, one of their guys (Hammersmith) leads off with a triple. Now, their bench is starting to zing it to me. 'We've got you now. It's all over.' Something like that. The next thing I know, Solarek comes out to the pitcher's circle and asks me if I knew where we were going to eat after the game. It broke the tension and they didn't score."

The newspaper accounts mention that Ty struck out 10 of the first 12 batters he faced. Since Wagner hit a double in the second, and Hammersmith, the opposing pitcher, hit a triple in the third, we must deduce that the next three batters went down on strikes. Given Ty's history in such situations, I would guess it was on nine pitches. I once asked him, "Why only nine?" His answer, "If I'm throwing that hard, why waste one?" He also takes into account that it is easier for the opposing team to score by wild pitch or passed ball in that situation than by any other means. The pitcher who throws strikes that can't be hit protects everybody from the hazards of the ball purposely thrown out of the strike zone.

The way that all of Ty's teammates and opponents remember it, Ty was one kind of pitcher with nobody on base, a second kind of pitcher with a runner on first, and a third kind of pitcher with a runner in scoring position. It might be helpful to go back to the 104.7 mph official clocking of his fastball. Ty will be the first to tell you that nobody throws their fastest pitch on every pitch if he wants

Bringing It Home

to stay in these extra-inning marathons. That pitch must be sitting on the shelf, however, ready for duty at all times.

Rocky calls it "second gear;" some people call it "taking over the game." We used to call it "reaching back for something extra." Whatever it's called, there is no mistaking the ferocity behind the effort. If the person is a grunter, the grunt will be heard that much more loudly. If the person normally takes a big step in the delivery, this step will be just that much bigger. The limits of personal comfort will be overcome in the service of getting the job done.

For Ty it was a matter of personal insult. It was his job as a pitcher to get you out. He saw it as your job to go back to the bench with a minimum of fuss. A 21-strikeout game every time would be just fine. If the strikeout didn't get the job done, then the batter was expected to make an easy out. Harder outs were remembered with a personal asterisk and a motto, "He shall pay."

Once an opposing player reached first base for any reason, Ty was offended. He made it his job to dispatch the rest of the lineup with as little fuss as possible. Sometimes three pitches, sometimes six, and sometimes nine completed the assignment that inning, but as far as he was concerned, it was his assignment. He would take over.

Here's where the ferocity kicks in again, but not just in his pitching. Anyone who ever saw him work with a runner on first base and less than two out remembers his fielding. He was the acknowledged best of his peers for a number of reasons: his rise ball was an extremely difficult pitch to bunt, he had an uncanny ability to race in quickly for a bunt, and he had a strong, accurate, overhand throw to all bases.

Since Ty was an acknowledged master at fielding the bunt, I asked him how he went about making the play. "I

Softball's Lefty Legend ~ Ty Stofflet

always ran in for the bunt and when I got it, turned for second or third, depending on where the lead runner was heading. More than 50% of the bunt throws I made were to the lead base, and I got most of them out."

Ronnie Kist, the catcher from New Jersey, was an elite bunter. His strategy throughout his career was to use his left-handed-hitting and speed and quickness to get on. "The problem with Ty," he said, "was that my strength was neutralized by his strength. With other pitchers, my job was to get the ball on the ground so the pitcher had to field it. That was enough for me to leg out a base hit and maybe cause an overthrow. With Ty, I was forced to hit to the other fielders. He was that good."

Okay, so getting to first base on Ty is a problem and getting to second base is a bigger problem. What if the player got into scoring position? How did Ty react? Have you ever sensed an intruder had entered your home with evil intent? Well, that's how Ty treated a runner on second base.

But what about third base and less than two out? Here, Ty built a personal furnace of fury intent on keeping this interloper from getting to Ty's "home." You see, home plate was not the batter's home plate; it was Ty's home plate. He owned it in the same way that defensive players in other sports defend their goal.

When an opposing player reached third base, Ty would invariably look at the interloper and acknowledge the accomplishment. "However," he would silently state, "that is the best you will do today, all day."

At those times when the unthinkable occurred and the other team scored, he became angrier. During this part of his career, one run is all his team expects him to need. "Ty will shut them down," has become a team credo. I do not

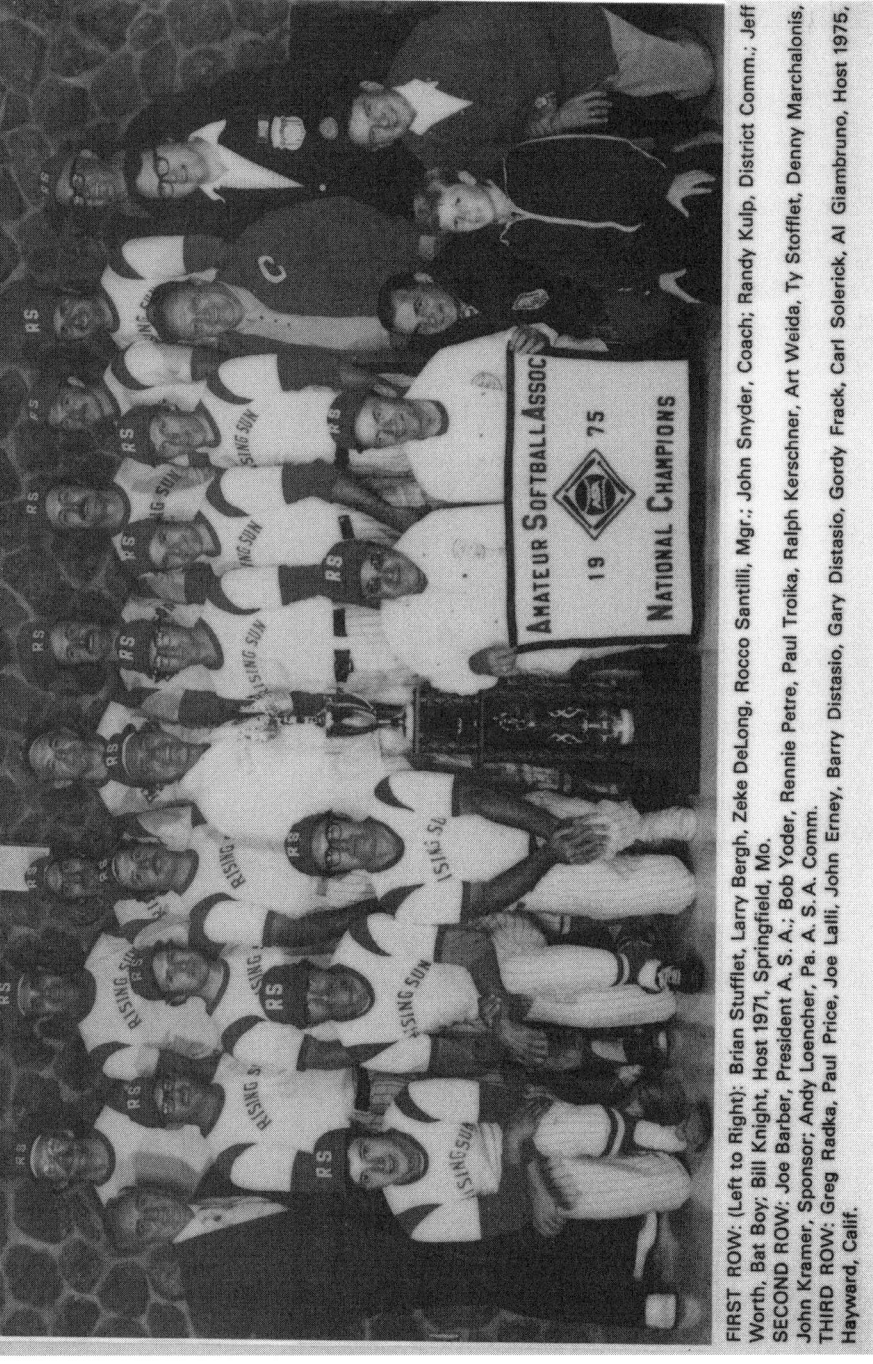

FIRST ROW: (Left to Right): Brian Stufflet, Larry Bergh, Zeke DeLong, Rocco Santilli, Mgr.; John Snyder, Coach; Randy Kulp, District Comm.; Jeff Worth, Bat Boy; Bill Knight, Host 1971, Springfield, Mo.
SECOND ROW: Joe Barber, President A. S. A.; Bob Yoder, Rennie Petre, Paul Troika, Ralph Kerschner, Art Weida, Ty Stofflet, Denny Marchalonis, John Kramer, Sponsor; Andy Loencher, Pa. A. S. A. Comm.
THIRD ROW: Greg Radka, Paul Price, Joe Lalli, John Erney, Barry Distasio, Gary Distasio, Gordy Frack, Carl Solerick, Al Giambruno, Host 1975, Hayward, Calif.

1975 - Team Picture

Softball's Lefty Legend ~ Ty Stofflet

know how many times they watched Ty strike out the side on nine pitches after a runner reached base, but Bob Lehman, who played against him before joining the Sunners in 1984, shared this strategy. "We were told never to stop at third base, for any reason, when he was throwing. There was no point to it. Something might happen with the throw to home. If you stopped at third, Ty was just going to leave you there."

Pay 'n Pak has taunted our ferocious gentleman and their lead runner has been left standing on third. That is their last serious threat in what turns out to be an 18-inning game. During the last eight innings, Ty is perfect. For the game he strikes out 32. Two Seattle pitchers split the 18 innings.

In only his third year in the nationals he already has two 30-plus strikeout games. There might be some advantage to being on a team that scores so late in games, if only that it affects the record books. His consecutive scoreless streak in the nationals now extends to 69 2/3 innings, the equivalent of 10 straight games.

In his next game, Ty faces Atlanta and strikes out the first 11 batters on the way to a 17-strikeout, one-hit performance. Reading had nine hits but plated only one run. The new Sunner hero is Zeke Delong, an outfielder who will later be called "the iceman" for his new team. Delong scores the run.

The manager is now being asked about his unhittable lefty flamethrower. After 76 2/3 scoreless innings, Rocky can't exactly just call him "good," so instead he allows that Ty has had a month of pitching the best he has ever seen him pitch. The first four games in the national have been Joe Lalli's idea of Sunners' hitless wonders softball. Lot's of action, but very few runs.

Bringing It Home

In the finals of the winners' bracket, Reading faces Aurora, IL, which manages to score a run in the first inning. This represents the first run allowed in 47 innings of competition in this year's national. In the third inning, the Rising Sun scores on a Zeke Delong RBI, which brings in Rennie Petre from second base.

Unless you are a softball purist, you might not appreciate the elegance of the eighth inning score that wins the game for Reading. Art Weida gets a single, which is misplayed, enabling him to go to second. Zeke Delong hits a sacrifice fly moving him to third. He comes home on a passed ball.

Softball is a game of opportunism. Players must react instinctively to situations that develop and end in an instant. The 60 feet between bases can be traveled in the moment a catcher is looking down at a ball near his feet. Try to be a little too fine and a pitch intended for just a little below and outside the corner of the strike zone may wind up behind the catcher.

Pressure creates opportunities and the Sunners know how to apply pressure. To the fans who know what they're observing, the runner who knows how to take that extra base, or turn a slightly misplayed ball into a run, is the catalyst that makes all the difference. Speed on the mound, at the plate, on the bases or in the field of play generates a level of excitement that can be sustained throughout an entire game. A final score of 2-1, no matter how the runs were scored, feels terrific to the winning team and its appreciative fans.

In the finals against Aurora, Ty gets to prove why he brought the other guys with him to the national, and his father, Harold, provides some insight into what was going on in his son's mind during the seventh inning.

Softball's Lefty Legend ~ Ty Stofflet

Reading scores one in the first and another in the third. Ty holds the Aurora team scoreless for the first six innings. In the seventh, Aurora puts together three hits, a walk, a rare misplay by Ty, and a sacrifice fly to score three runs and go ahead, 3-2.

This is where softball proves that it is the team that wins or loses. Stofflet has finished his seven innings and he is the losing pitcher of record. He will not throw another pitch in this game and yet, when his team scores two runs in the bottom of the seventh inning, he is now the pitcher of record on the winning side.

Dick Brubaker, the losing pitcher, as the saying goes, deserved a better fate, but with a couple of errors and some opportunism shown by Reading, the Sunners get back two for the win. Final score, 4-3. Ty is the quintessence of the grateful teammate as he states that it takes everybody to win a game as that victory just proved.

Regarding the three runs in the seventh inning, Harold Stofflet, who saw most of Ty's key games throughout his career, remembers talking to Ty. "He got into the seventh inning and stopped playing the game a pitch at a time. He could see the prize and it dazzled him."

Here, on the brink of gaining clear softball dominance, Ty makes a few missteps, but with poetic justice, the hitless wonders keep finding a way to get just one more run than their opponent.

Speaking of poetic justice, listen to Rocky Santilli upon returning home. "So I pull into the driveway and drop my bags on the porch. Before going into the house, I drove to the Reading newspaper and I said, 'The kook is here, except now he has won the national championship. Are you going to send anybody along to New Zealand for the World Championship?' Well, the guy didn't have a clue; he was stuttering."

Bringing It Home

And it is time to look at our third player in crisis at the end of 1974, Carl Solarek. During Ty's consecutive-game shutout streak he has allowed no passed balls. In fact, his stellar offense and defense in this tournament have earned him a first team All-American designation on the All-Tournament team. Three other Reading players make first team – shortstop Gary Distasio, utility player Art Weida, and Ty Stofflet. Second baseman Joe Lalli and utility player Bob Yoder earn second-team honors.

For the third time in three nationals, Ty is voted the Most Valuable Player in the tournament. Counting the ASA and the ISC together, he has had an incredible run. In his last six major tournaments, either under ISC or ASA sanction, Ty has taken home six MVP trophies. However, as we continue to learn about Ty, one can only ask what he will do at the next level when he gets to represent his country as the lone American team in the competition.

America's Team

THE RISING SUN TEAM MAKES an inauspicious start on its way to the world championship in New Zealand. Rocky is not so much offended at having to raise money to cross the Pacific. That has been a fact of life for his entire managerial career. He is offended because he can't get access to a proper fieldhouse and must use the local gyms. From his perspective, competing teams should be given the proper support and accommodations.

The games are scheduled for the end of January through February 8th, summer in the Southern Hemisphere. The last thing he wants is to be shaking off the cobwebs while the other teams are in midsummer form. But they will be going to represent the USA and they are confident of their chances.

Seven nations are represented: United States, Canada, New Zealand, Japan, Taiwan, Guam and South Africa. Because the games are in the Pacific, teams from the Dominican Republic, Mexico, Puerto Rico, the Virgin Islands and the Bahamas have decided not to participate. The presence of Canada, a perennial world softball power, and New Zealand, with its top right-hander Kevin Herlihy, however, guarantee to make this a world-class event.

The three best teams are the United States, Canada and New Zealand. Japan ranks somewhere in the middle, with the other three nations filling in the competition.

Softball's Lefty Legend ~ Ty Stofflet

The prior International Softball Federation World Championship, held in Manila, ended with Canada in first place with a 10-1 record, the United States in second (9-3), and New Zealand third (7-4). When interviewed by a local paper prior to the tournament, Ty is quite forthcoming. "From what I've seen and heard, I don't think we'll lose a game."

This is a 34-year-old man at the height of his softball powers. He has a U.S. team that includes Carl Walker, the nation's top hitter, behind him and he feels ultra-confident about his team's chances. He has also made a life choice that is consistent with the deepest level of his personality. He has decided that one way or another, his softball fate will be entwined with that of the Sunners.

By this time, he has been wooed by anyone with a job to offer and a softball team to join. In private meetings, he has learned without exception the value others place on his skills. But he has forged an agreement with Rocky that works for both men. He gets to play softball around the world, and still remain faithful to his stay-at-home values. From his Allentown-Reading view of the world, he might be invisible to many in his hometown as a pitcher, but he is never overlooked as a person.

He has also joined the ranks of "best pitchers in the country," an extremely exclusive club. In the '70s, about 100,000 players are registered in fast pitch softball, but only a handful of pitchers are perched at the top. His recent play at the nationals constitutes a personal statement of intent to dominate and it would be foolish for him to indicate any feeling other than confidence whenever he goes to the mound.

After a couple of wins over Japan, the U.S. team faces Canada. The matchup is Stofflet versus Stan Kern, and

America's Team

Kern hits Ty in his left arm, causing it to go numb for about 10 minutes. "Rocky wanted to take me out, but I told him to wait and went to first base. It took quite some time to get feeling back in the arm. I was worried."

Later in the game, Kern came to bat and Ty tells this story. "I have spent my entire career as a guy who would not throw to hurt anybody on purpose. But the fans had warned me before the game that I had better watch out. I was going down. And then I get hit right on the pitching arm. So, he comes to the plate, and for the first time in my life I am not sure what to do. But in the end I decide that physically hurting someone else as part of a softball game is just wrong."

Since that is the closest he ever came to using his throwing arm as a purposeful weapon, we can say with confidence that his entire career did not include the "hurt 'em" ball. And that is how one earns the label, "tough but not mean."

The U.S. loses to Canada in 10 innings, 1-0. Ty is not sharp in the 10th inning, and the winning hit comes after a dropped foul ball. Later in the first scheduled game against New Zealand, he throws a three-hit shutout over eight innings, striking out 17. In the eighth, his triple knocks in the only run of the game. This is Ty's second game-winner of the tournament. Earlier, against South Africa, his sacrifice fly in the 12th inning brings home Yoder with the winning run.

As the tournament continues, the U.S. gets a break when New Zealand beats Canada, 2-1, putting Rising Sun, Canada and New Zealand in a 6-1 deadlock at the top of the international standings. After Larry Bergh tosses a one-hitter against Guam (4-0), the stage is set for what will forever be regarded as the best game of Ty's career.

Bill Plummer III, who has developed international

Softball's Lefty Legend ~ Ty Stofflet

softball relationships in his role as manager of the National Softball Hall of Fame, has put together an account with contributions from both sides of the world. After 28 years, he was able to round up a number of players and others who had a hand in that day's events and have contributed to his story. It is with considerable pleasure that we offer his account of THE GAME.

A Fast Pitch Game for the Ages

by Bill Plummer III

The date: February 4, 1976, in Lower Hutt, New Zealand.

That's when Ty Stofflet and Kevin Herlihy opposed each other in a game of fast pitch softball that defied imagination.

Who would have imagined that Stofflet and Herlihy, both in the prime of their careers, would combine to strike out 52?

But they did!

Who would have imagined that Stofflet would hurl a 20-inning no-hitter?

But he did!

Who would have imagined that Stofflet would retire 56 batters consecutively before hitting a batter with a changeup?

But he did!

Who would have imagined that Stofflet would drive in the winning run for the third consecutive game?

But he did, smacking a two-out single to center field in the top of the 20th inning, scoring Paul Troika, who had gone in to run for Paul Price.

Herlihy had given Price a leadoff walk, and struck out the next batter. With pinch runner Troika on first base and one out, a grounder was hit to second baseman Wayne

Softball's Lefty Legend ~ Ty Stofflet

Baldwin. Seeing the grounder, Troika ran to within five feet of Baldwin and backpedaled. Obviously surprised by Troika's base running ploy, Baldwin threw to first instead of second, allowing Troika to scamper into second standing up.

"I learned that base running ploy in elementary school softball and it paid off 20 years later," recalled Troika. "Ty, of course, was the hero and I was part of softball history."

Who would have imagined that the two pitchers would hurl the equivalent of almost three games?

But they did!

It was a softball game beyond all games and one of the most incredible games pitched in the history of fast pitch softball.

In the history of the International Softball Federation, it ranks, without question, as the greatest game ever pitched in men's world championship play, which started in 1966.

Anyone involved in softball at the time figured the meeting between Stofflet and Herlihy would be a game for the softball history books and one to remember.

After all, the two pitchers were in the prime of their careers and each team was counting on its ace to deliver a game to remember, perhaps even the best game of their respective careers, to keep their teams in the hunt for the gold medal.

As expected, neither pitcher gave an inch. It was a game that helped put Herlihy on the softball map pitching against the legendary left-hander from Coplay, PA.

"That fact that I was able to play against a guy as great as Ty made it that much more memorable," Herlihy said. "That set up my own reputation over here [in the USA] and I have been able to build on it.

"I believe that game more than any other set up my rep-

A Fast Pitch Game for the Ages

utation as one of the world's best pitchers. It certainly gave me the confidence to eventually accept an offer to play in the USA."

Although Stofflet said it was the greatest game he ever pitched, Herlihy had a different reaction. "To say it was the best game I ever pitched is debatable. However, it is the one game that I will remember more than any other. It had been billed as the best left-hander in the world versus the best right-hander at the time. I believe it lived up to and exceeded all expectations."

Neither pitcher tired and players know or accept that with two pitchers of this caliber, the game could have gone on forever.

"In long-inning games such as this one, I think once you get past 10 innings or so, adrenaline takes over," Herlihy said. "The batters almost resolve themselves to the fact that the game will go on forever, and fatigue never comes into it. The next day is when the tiredness set in."

Herlihy didn't care how long the game would go. "It's a rare opportunity to be able to be part of such a wonderful experience. I will always remember Rocky Santilli's (USA manager) words to me around the 16th inning as he walked back across the diamond from the third-base coaching box. 'Why don't you and Ty go across to Somes Island (a small island in the middle of Wellington Harbour) and battle this between the two of you and let the rest of us go home to bed?'

"What I remember most was the build-up immediately before the game," continued Herlihy. "You could sense the huge home crowd had a sixth sense that something special was about to unfold. As the national anthem was played, I felt the hairs on the back of my neck rise. It was certainly very special that such a game could be played in front of my hometown crowd.

Softball's Lefty Legend ~ Ty Stofflet

"I will also remember the USA team in particular being able to pitch against the legendary Carl Walker and that night get the better of him. I also remember Ty's fantastic pitching performance in pitching a no-hitter. Without a doubt it was the most complete game I have ever witnessed in my entire career. I guess there was always going to be one winner, yet while disappointed that we lost on an error from a hit of Ty's, on reflection I can only feel pride in my personal performance and the personal duel within the game between Ty and myself."

Herlihy ended up losing by the narrowest of margins, 1-0, but hurled an outstanding game himself – allowing five hits and striking out 20. The fifth hit, however, was Stofflet's single in the top of the 20th inning that brought across Troika with the game's only run. It was Stofflet's second hit of the game.

Stofflet retired the first 56 batters before No. 57 (Basil McLean) was hit by a pitch to end the streak of perfect pitching at 18 2/3 innings.

Although McLean was the only New Zealand base runner, Stofflet felt McLean should have never reached base. "The sad thing about it is that pitch was a strike on the inside corner. The batter (McLean) just stuck his wrist out, wanting to get hit. It was a crummy thing to do, but I guess they were just desperate to get a man on base."

Rocky Santilli, USA manager, also felt the same as his outstanding left-hander.

"I thought it was a strike. They were not used to a pitch (changeup) like that back then. He leaned into the pitch and got caught," said Santilli. "It was a strike then and still is a strike now. If I had been umpiring, he wouldn't have gotten a base.

"I was trying to preserve the perfect game," continued

A Fast Pitch Game for the Ages

Santilli. "You look for a break and you hope the breaks go your way."

Carl Solarek, the USA catcher, was on the receiving end of the pitch and felt McLean "leaned into the pitch."

"He turned into it, a changeup, and it was a natural reaction," said Solarek, who conferred with Santilli after the pitch.

Santilli asked the umpire if McLean attempted to get out of the way of the pitch. The umpire said he did, which is a judgment call and can't be protested.

McLean, however, never got past first base. Stofflet struck out the next batter to retire the side.

After the USA scored in the 20th, Stofflet set the Kiwi down in 1-2-3 fashion and finished with 32 strikeouts. The USA stranded 13 runners.

Stofflet (then 34) couldn't believe the accomplishment.

"I can't believe it myself," Ty told Gordon Smith, sports editor of the *Evening Chronicle*. "It's the most unbelievable accomplishment of my career. And to do it in international competition – oh, I can't believe this has happened to me!"

Was it the greatest game Stofflet ever pitched in his almost legendary career?

"Yes, no question about it," Stofflet said. "That day I had command of all my pitches. Some days you'll have one or two that aren't working. Or I might be rushing. That day it seemed I was supposed to win. Everything worked like a dream. Everything went the way it was supposed to go.

"I was still strong at the end," continued Stofflet. "I wasn't tired and I had the ball moving real good. I had some candy bars before the game and during the game, so they might have given me more stamina."

It was the first time Stofflet and Herlihy had faced each

Softball's Lefty Legend ~ Ty Stofflet

other, although they had heard of one another, and each would go on to establish himself as a great pitcher in his country.

For Stofflet, the 1976 World Championship was the only one in which he would ever participate, although he was selected for the 1980 USA Team but had to decline because of a wrist injury.

Herlihy, however, went on the play in more ISF World Championships, winning a record 20 games.

Besides the ISF game, Stofflet and Herlihy would face each other five more times during their careers and "that game set the tone for future personal duels between Ty and myself," Herlihy said.

The next time the two met, Herlihy was pitching for the Saginaw Bolters, and the game went 14 innings with Kevin winning, 1-0. That game was on a Saturday, and the two met again Sunday morning when Ty won, 1-0.

"I played Ty another three times, one went nine innings (1-0, of course) and the other two we split in regulation innings," said Herlihy, who works as an advertising account manager for the radio network in Hamilton, New Zealand. "No other pitcher ever commanded that same feeling as the times I played against Ty. Within each and every game there was a second duel taking place between the two of us, all stemming from that first and most fantastic game of them all in 1976 in Lower Hutt.

"I believe that game more than any other set up my reputation as one of the world's best pitchers," said Herlihy.

Rocky Santilli, the USA manager and Stofflet's manager during the regular season, said, "What can you say about a game like this? It comes around once every 50 or 100 years. It doesn't get any better than this. Under the circumstances (playing in a World Championship with two of the

A Fast Pitch Game for the Ages

game's best pitchers), you had to wonder if it was ever going to end."

The more than 8,000 people attending the game probably wondered the same thing as the two titans of fast pitch softball matched pitch after pitch in a game that lasted four hours and 20 minutes.

"Neither one (pitcher) slowed up," said Santilli. "They just kept going and going."

Both pitchers were in the prime of their careers and the last thing either pitcher wanted to do was to show any signs of letting up. Neither did.

Solarek said Stofflet got stronger each inning. "You could see it in his eyes. I have never caught a game that long, that perfect," said Solarek, who played minor league baseball in the Detroit Tigers' farm system for five years before turning to softball. The last two years of his baseball career Solarek played at the "AA" level.

A 1980 graduate of Penn State, Solarek played only one year of Class "A" fast pitch before starting to catch Ty, which he said was easy. "He threw hard and was consistently around the plate," said Solarek, who earned four All-America selections during his career.

Unlike some pitchers who couldn't pitch game after game, Stofflet kept himself in outstanding shape and "could pitch day after day." Besides the blazing speed and back-breaking change-up, Stofflet also had a knuckleball, which "you couldn't catch."

If you were going to beat Stofflet, you would have to get to him early. With him, one run would be enough to win a game. Even if a runner reached third against him, getting him home wasn't automatic.

"Ty would put it into another gear (when a runner got to third)," said Santilli. "I would gauge the real good pitchers that way. How successful they were with runners on third base and less than two out."

Time and time again, Stofflet would reach back for that something extra and throw six or nine pitches to retire the side on strikes and leave batters going back to the dugout with a look of dismay or utter frustration on their face.

When all was said and done, neither Stofflet nor Herlihy would face each other again in ISF World Championship play.

Mother Nature had other plans for the event, the arrival of the monsoon forcing the end of the competition and Canada, the USA, and New Zealand declared tri-champions by the ISF, as then-ISF President W.W. (Bill) Kethan announced.

"There was no other way to do it," said Kethan. "In fairness to all the teams, the three teams who had not been eliminated from the series had to share the title."

Kevin "Chick" Baldwin, who was the organizer of the World Championship, said "extensive plans were made to re-organize all the Canadian and U.S. travel. Then we re-booked their accommodation in Fiji and Honolulu, but the Canadians would not cooperate.

"The U.S. team boss (former ASA president Andy Pendergast) was happy to stay the extra day to play the final but the Canadians wanted $10,000. At that time it was a very expensive demand. We refused and the world championship was shared."

The USA and Canada felt they were the two best teams but never got to prove it. The Canadian team was so upset with the decision that it walked out at the awards dinner when the decision was announced by the ISF.

"Kevin Baldwin of New Zealand gave us the trophy

A Fast Pitch Game for the Ages

but said not to show it to anyone and that they would get another one for New Zealand and Canada," said USA's Santilli.

"You see, the New Zealand people look at things differently than we do. To New Zealand, winning isn't everything. When we beat them in that 20-inning game, we returned to the hotels in the same bus. They were singing and having a good time. You would have thought they won the game."

The USA finished with an 11-2 record with Stofflet 4-2, George Ulmer 4-0 and Larry Bergh 3-0.

A former basketball player for the Pittsburgh Pipers of the ABA, the 6-7 Bergh called **THE GAME** "the best I've ever seen. It was a fun game to watch with two of the best [pitchers] in the world. It was a fantastic game."

Although the teams didn't get to prove which was the best, Stofflet and Herlihy proved themselves in the fast pitch game for the ages. There may never be another game like this.

....

After the win against New Zealand, the next important matchup pits the U.S. against Canada again, with Stofflet facing Pete Landers. The game started with an error. With two out and two on, McMillan tripled. Both runs were unearned but were enough to win as the U.S. managed only one run in the fifth. Ty is now 3-2 with a 0.00 ERA. In 52 innings he has struck out 86, and walked only four.

The Sunners finish the first round in second place and will again face the Canadians in the semi-finals. Rocky is satisfied, his team is poised to face their northern neighbors and

1976 - Team Picture

A Fast Pitch Game for the Ages

his ace is smarting from a couple of losses that must be avenged.

In the semifinal game between the USA and Canada, cream rises to the top. The world's best pitcher and best hitter have come to display their talents. Stofflet throws a two-hit shutout, striking out 12. Carl Walker hits a homerun in the sixth. That was all the scoring and all the U.S. needed.

Now the U.S. waits for the results of the Canada-New Zealand game to determine its opponent for the championship. And that is where the softball gods decided to end the tournament. No, not the officials who preside over the games or even the players and managers who get onto the field, but the real softball deities, the ones that control the weather. Monsoon 9, ISF Teams 0. And so the team results are considered a draw, with the U.S., Canada and New Zealand declared tri-champions.

The decision about the individual champion of the games was no contest. Ty Stofflet was declared both the best pitcher and the best player in the tournament. He had 98 strikeouts, 15 more than Herlihy's record of 72 set in 1972. His ERA was flawless and his 20-inning no-hitter/disputed perfect game was the best single-game performance ever recorded in ISF world play.

In addition, he contributed three game-winning hits, each in extra innings, the eighth, the 12th, and, most emphatically, the 20th. In Ty's trophy case are two jade-based penholders standing less than a foot high. They are dwarfed by the collection of local, state, regional and national trophies that are by-products of his continuing excellence. If you ask him which trophies mean the most to him, he has no trouble pointing out these twins of international achievement.

Ty with his ISF Jade Trophies ~ 2004
Most Valuable Player • Most Valuable Pitcher

After the Ball Is Over

THE WRITER, OSCAR WILDE, is credited with the statement, "There are only two problems in life, not getting what you want and getting it." Rocky is now a manager who is returning to Leesport after shocking the locals by being the national champion and, within six months of that feat, being one of three International Softball Federation tri-champions. He has the best pitcher in 1975-76 and, to top everything, this year's ASA National will essentially be a set of home games.

No, they didn't put the championship in Leesport, but through the efforts of chairman Earl Hunsicker, a new Bicentennial ballpark has been built in nearby Allentown. That stadium, combined with the already established Patriots Park, makes Allentown an attractive location for the ASA's major championship event.

Santilli has also been busy finding a sponsor and putting together a playing schedule fitting the elevated status of his championship team. He refuses to stop playing local teams just because the Sunners are the current champs. He believes that it helps everyone concerned to have his team in the local competitions as well as the travel tournaments.

The new sponsor is Billard Barbell, whose president, Abe Goodman, will be helping establish the Reading club as a substantial force in the softball world. The team will be called the Billard Sunners to demonstrate a measure of respect for the reputation amassed by the Rising Sun Hotel, and John Kramer, its owner, during its 22-year history in Pennsylvania softball.

Softball's Lefty Legend ~ Ty Stofflet

This year will include a number of trips, including those to Springfield, MO; Cedar Rapids, IA; Victoria, British Columbia; Stratford, CT; Boston and Worcester, MA; Bermuda; Poughkeepsie, NY; Fair Lawn and Parsippany, NJ; Philadelphia and Allentown, PA, the site of the ASA 1976 National Major.

In addition to an expanded schedule and the title of reigning national champion, they have added a new first baseman, Jeff Seip. Seip has been on Santilli's "must have" list for the past five years, but he remained an Allentown Patriot. This year, he asked Rocky if he could join the team and is immediately accepted and written in at No. 3 in the batting order

When you consider that Seip has never been to a national tournament and is joining a team that has recently been crowned twice, his move to the third spot in the lineup might seem odd. If you have ever seen Seip hit or heard about his prowess with the bat, however, there would be no question.

Seip joins the Billard Sunners at age 23, but he had already been playing in the local men's leagues since he was 13. "When I was 15, it just clicked. I hit two home runs in one game and never stopped hitting. It happened for some reason. I'm not sure why but we were playing a home game and I started to hit."

One of the reasons that Seip was such a great hitter has to do with the gift of extraordinary eyesight. "I have eyes like Ted Williams. I can see objects at a mile that people with normal vision can't see until they're a half mile away." His 20/10 eyesight is coupled with an ability to be disciplined at the plate. When he came to the Sunners, he knew that others batting behind him could drive him in if he drew a walk. He rarely swung at bad pitches.

After the Ball Is Over

I asked him what it was like facing Ty during his five years with the Patriots. "Not much fun really because you couldn't see the ball. He threw 100 mph and he had every pitch in the book – the riseball, the drop and the change-up really killed you. The exceptional pitchers could throw the changeup with the same exact motion without slowing their arm or changing what they did on the other pitches.

"If I studied a pitcher, I could pick up pitches by looking at how he held a ball in his glove. You just couldn't tell with Ty, you had to guess."

When asked about his success against Ty, he said, "After a season against him, I started to do a little better. Every now and then, he'd let me hit the ball. He'd throw it where I was swinging. It wasn't too often. Nobody had much success against him. I believe that he was the best pitcher that ever walked on the mound."

It is important to remember that great hitters and great pitchers, in their heart of hearts, always believe that they can win any confrontation. He recalled a game against Ty that stands out. "One of the years we played in the July 4th Allentown tournament, I was playing first base. Ty reached first by a hit or walk He was just shutting us out that game and, jokingly, I said to him, 'Hey, you better be careful. I'm gonna' hit a home run off you next time.' So he looked back at me and he says, 'You couldn't hit a ball off me if I threw right-handed.'"

"Okay, so I just laughed. Wouldn't you know it, the next time up I hit a home run off him. So I'm goin' around the bases and I'm razzing him a little bit, which continues the joke that we had started. Well, it turned into a situation which wasn't funny anymore, because the Sunners thought that I was hotdogging. They started yelling at me. It got pretty nasty."

"I told everybody afterward what had happened. It

Softball's Lefty Legend ~ Ty Stofflet

started off being a joke, but when it was all said and done, it didn't end that way. Ty wasn't too happy because he thought I was showing him up. But we worked it out once we talked about it. That's the game I'll never forget because it just worked out. I said what I said, he said what he said, and I did hit one the very next time up. We laugh about it now but it was tense."

Jeff Seip is now a Billard Sunner, and his impact is immediate. He is a high average, power hitter who adds a measure of intimidation that will be matched by only a few players throughout softball in his era. If you ask Ty to rate the two best he saw in his time, he points to Carl Walker, whom the Sunners took to New Zealand, and Jeff Seip, his new teammate.

This is the post-championship year so the Billard Sunners are receiving considerably more press coverage, the kind of press that now contains a sportswriter's byline. Most past coverage of the team appears without a byline, indicating that team officials usually communicated game scores and statistics to the newspaper. This year, everything the Billard Sunners do receives attention in the newspaper.

By July 4th, Ty owns a 21-3 record, which includes his latest no-hitter, against Raybestos. In a July 3rd doubleheader, he beats the Connecticut team, 2-0, and Larry Bergh completes the sweep, 3-0. In his account of the game in the *Bridgeport Sunday Post*, Peter Putrimas includes the following quotes from Ty, "I gotta admit I was pretty sharp tonight. The riser was really working. All I did was rear back and throw as hard as I could."

In his no-hitter, with the bases loaded on two walks and an error, Stofflet strikes out the opponent's best hitter, Vinnie Caserto, on three risers. "I just said to myself to keep firin' away and make him hit my best pitch." In winning this game, Ty beats Hall of Famer Al Lewis. Ty's comment is politically correct. "It's always a treat when I beat a guy like Al Lewis, especially with a no-hitter."

At this point in the season, Reading has a 41-4 record. Reading plays a doubleheader with Raybestos the next day and allows their third pitcher, John Erney, to throw the last game after winning the first three. Raybestos wins the meaningless game, 12-3.

The following week the Sunners go to Worcester, MA, and get back to serious business. Larry Bergh loses the first game, 2-0, and Stofflet wins the second, 1-0. He has 12 strikeouts. On the second day, Ty wins the first game, 7-2. John Erney loses the second, 7-5.

The fun highlight of the championship summer season is a scheduled three-day weekend series against a team of 1975 National ASA All-Stars. Jeff Seip is leading the team in batting (.370), home runs (20), hits (53) and RBI (49). The starting lineup against the National All-Stars will be: 1) Lalli (2b), 2) Yoder (cf), 3) Seip (1b), 4) Delong (rf), 5) Price (3b), 6) G. Distasio (ss), 7) Weida (lf) and 8) Solarek (c).

The All-Stars are a wrecking crew managed by Cliff Smith of Aurora, IL. Carl Walker, Tom Wagner, Tom Penders (yes, the long-time Texas basketball head coach), Abe "Home Run" Baker, Billy Stewart, Bill Pfeiffer, Al Lewis and Dick Brubaker, among others, have come for some friendly weekend competition.

The five-game competition ends, 3-2, All-Stars. They win the first two games on Friday, roughing up Ty and his team for six runs. When interviewed afterward, Smith makes the point that the All-Star team worked hard not to chase Stofflet's riser. Their goal was to get Stofflet to bring the ball down. After a low-scoring four innings, the All-

Softball's Lefty Legend ~ Ty Stofflet

Stars get the Sunners to throw the ball around a little. Wagner finishes matters with a two-run single.

The next day, with the same lineup, Ty throws a one-hit shutout, 4-0. Bergh and the Sunners lose the next game, 7-3. After giving up six runs, Larry is ejected for an act that most pitchers would have liked to experience once, but have never summoned up the nerve to try. The umpire gives him a ball that he feels is too heavy. So on the next pitch he heaves the ball out of the stadium behind third base and is thrown out of the game. Bergh said, "I was asked why I didn't throw it over the backstop. I figured if I threw it there, they would only throw it back in."

For the final game of the week on Sunday, Ty draws the nod from Santilli. He throws five shutout innings and the Sunners win, 8-0, but the damage has been done. Bragging rights belong to the All-Stars. Ty calls the first game of the match "the worst game of my life" and blames it on not enough weekday work in the City League. He vows not to make that mistake again.

As of August 18th, Ty has amassed a 31-5 record, with 23 earned runs, 500 strikeouts and 57 walks in 265 innings. His team is 65-11. All of this preliminary play has been entertaining and the travel has been interesting. Now the true season begins.

In the first game of the 1976 ASA National, the Billard Sunners draw Aurora, the runner-up from the prior year. This might be very good or disastrous, since one of these powerhouse teams will be heading to the losers' bracket. Aurora's Dick Brubaker throws a three-hit shutout. Ty gives up one less hit, but unfortunately one of the hits is a two-run home run by Darryl Day. Reading, in front of its home fans, is sent to the losers' bracket. They must win the next nine games in order to repeat.

After the Ball Is Over

In their first game in the losers' bracket, Larry Bergh and his teammates win a 14-0 laugher. In addition to throwing a shutout, Bergh hits two home runs. Next, Ty pitches a no-hitter against Oklahoma City. Barry Distasio, who entered as a pinch runner, hit a bottom of the seventh, walk-off grand slam for Reading. The final score is 4-0. Ty is just as thrilled with this no-hitter as he has been with the other four in national competition.

In their third losers' bracket test, the Sunners face Sunnyvale, CA, and appear to be on the ropes from the very start. Ty gives up a leadoff triple, but strands the runner. In the sixth, Sunnyvale puts together a single and another triple to score its only run. In the seventh, Ty reaches with a single, Yoder scores him with a double and Price brings Yoder home with a game-winning single.

The next game, pitting Stofflet's Sunners against Roy Burlison's Springfield, MO, team, features two of the nation's top pitchers. But according to Ty in the Reading newspaper, the umpires cost Burlison the game in the seventh, 1-0. Umpires call a total of 11 illegal pitches against Burlison. An illegal pitch results in an automatic ball, and also advances any runners one base.

In Dave Kutch's Sept. 16th *Reading Eagle* story, Ty says, "The umps should leave the pitchers alone. Slow pitch is killing the fast pitch game quickly enough. With 85% of today's softball being slow pitch, there are no good young pitchers coming along. Now the umps' calls on the pitchers become more technical, and it's hurting the pitchers that are left. This will kill the game even faster. Burlison's a good friend and I'm sorry to see this happen to him."

So Stofflet beats Burlison, 1-0, and he feels no joy at all. It is a hollow experience because the umpires, not his team, made the difference. The measure of a man is

Softball's Lefty Legend ~ Ty Stofflet

whether he feels the same about rules when they work for or against him. Here is a "technicality" that has worked for the Sunners and it makes Ty sad for what it means to the future of this sport he loves.

In what turns out to be the Sunners' final game, they meet Detroit. Ty gets one of his team's two hits as the Sunners are shut out. Detroit, with Carl Walker playing first base, scratches out two runs, one on a delayed squeeze play that scores Walker. The Detroit team is particularly pleased because they have defeated the best.

The Sunners have had a great barnstorming season, but in the end, Brubaker and Aurora have ruined the homecoming party the Billard Sunners had planned for Allentown. If the fans expect to see another championship, they're going to need to go to next year's national in Midland, MI.

Remember the three out of four games the Sunners won against Raybestos? What a difference a month makes. The Raybestos Cardinals defeat Aurora and go on to win the 1976 national championship.

The Gang's All Here
Let's Have a Party

ROCKY SANTILLI HAD A FEELING during the national that his team was not as sharp as they had been in New Zealand. And one thing he knew for sure: let up even a little on these other teams, and you open the door for misery. But he didn't have to preach that point at the beginning of the new season; his team has had a year to feel what it was like to finish an also-ran fifth.

Dick Brubaker, putting together a 3-0 shutout to open the national and a second-game win against Stofflet in the Billard-All-Stars series, has identified himself as a pitcher who knows how to beat Reading. His Aurora, IL, team has finished second and is struggling with what it will take to bring the championship trophy home this year. The Sunners must be thinking that the road to the national will have to go through Aurora.

At another level, however, the 1976 team was stronger than previous teams, if only for the fact that the middle of Rocky's lineup is very powerful and the team has not had to have an extended season that started in January and concluded in September. For this group of amateurs, softball in 1976 seemed like a fulltime job.

At the beginning of the season, Rocky believes the team is more relaxed. He has chalked up last year's problems (which surfaced at the All-Star series) as "peaking early" and does not foresee those same problems this year.

Softball's Lefty Legend ~ Ty Stofflet

He has decided to take a positive view toward the team's preparation, focusing on the idea that a relaxed juggernaut makes an unbeatable foe.

This year's schedule includes the state qualifier in August, and the national tournament in Midland, MI, in September. Overall, the schedule is not nearly as taxing, with most games either local or the Eastern Seaboard League.

National qualifying rules now provide two ways for the Sunners to reach the tournament – winning the Pennsylvania State Championship for an automatic berth, or, failing that, winning the regional in Fox Hill, VA.

The 1977 team's basic lineup is quite familiar: Stofflet, Bergh and Erney pitching; Carl Solarek, catching; Jeff Seip, first base; Joe Lalli, second base; Gary Distasio, shortstop; Bobby Yoder, third base; Art Weida, left field; Barry Distasio, center field; and Zeke Delong, right field.

The Sunners start slowly. Ty's early record is 3-2, but this is the year to build momentum and not peak too early. Worcester, MA, beats him twice in May, 2-1 and 1-0. But Billard goes to the Lancaster Memorial tournament and wins five games in a row to take the title. There is little fanfare here, in the same way that Major League Baseball players don't get too excited about wins and losses in the early summer. What's important is to be where you need to be when the season is on the line. Ty is now 8-2 and is voted MVP of the Lancaster Tournament.

On June 6th, Barry Parmer and York Barbell beat Ty and the Sunners, 1-0. But on June 18th and 19th, the Billard Sunners beat the National Champion Raybestos Cardinals four games in a row. The Sunners are 23-5.

By June 25th, the Sunners have an 11-game winning streak. On June 27th, the Sunners beat Sam Ardolino, the

The Gang's All Here

New Jersey pitcher who stoked my curiosity about Ty, 1-0. His team, IHOP, lost all four games, with Ty pitching a couple of innings in each. Bergh and Erney completed most of the action.

The July 4th tournament in Allentown has a new format. Each team will play nine games, scoring a point for a win and a half-point for a seven-inning tie. The team with the highest point total will be the winner.

During tournaments, the crowd at a Stofflet game waits in anticipation for those moments when Ty must rear back and take over the game. It is then that they can state, without reservation, that they saw him at his fastest. Fans standing behind Tiger Woods when he pulls out the driver, or those watching Michael Jordan with the ball, one point down and a few seconds remaining, have known that feeling. The anticipation is breathtaking.

Against F & M Bankers of Virginia, such a moment occurs. In the third inning, they start with first and third and no out. The all-knowing crowd is murmuring something like, "Watch this!" and craning their necks to make sure they get a glimpse of human perfection. Today they are not disappointed. Ty overmatches the next three hitters with fastball after fastball. In the seventh, the Sunners get a run to win, 1-0.

When asked afterwards how he accomplished that feat, he said by throwing as fast as he could. "The crowd saw my fastest that evening." The other team has taken him to his top level, but the only ones entertained are the fans. How can you get satisfaction from having made your opponent's ace work his hardest to beat you, when the results confirm that you were over-matched in the first place?

On August 8th, the Sunners play an exhibition game

Softball's Lefty Legend ~ Ty Stofflet

against baseball's Minor League Reading "AA" Phillies. The rules of softball are in play when the Sunners are in the field, the rules of hardball apply when the Phils are in the field.

In three innings, Ty strikes out seven and walks two. Interestingly, both Stofflet and Seip get hits against a bona fide Minor League pitcher. The Sunners win, 1-0, as the hardball players acknowledge that trying to hit a 100 mph riser mixed in with a dipsy doodle changeup should be declared unfair.

Having watched a number of minor leaguers who also played softball, it is ironic to me that neither Ty Stofflet nor Jeff Seip ever gave baseball much of a chance. I am not sure how many other great softball players might have been good major leaguers if they had stuck it out in the minors. I am positive that the skills demonstrated by Ty and Jeff would have lent themselves for real possibilities for mainstream baseball success. I'm pretty sure that Davey Lopes agrees with me.

The fun and games of the 1977 season are over as the Pennsylvania State "AA" Tournament approaches on August 12th. The games are on the line so it is time for Ty to take center stage and dominate.

In the opener, Reading's Larry Bergh, who is 21-1, beats Allentown on a one-hitter, 7-0. Delong and Seip hit home runs.

Ty's first tournament game is against McNelis and York. Ty strikes out the first 11 batters he faces and 18 in seven innings, no-hitting York. Zeke Delong, batting cleanup, hits a sacrifice fly. End of scoring, end of game. If the Sunners peaked too early last year, this year Stofflet is showing that he will insure that their timing is just right.

The final game is against York. This time the score is 4-

The Gang's All Here

0, Sunners. The team with a lot to prove has started out just as planned. This is a methodical victory. Ty throws a two-hitter and breezes with 11 strikeouts, allowing two singles and no walks.

Ty's interview by Ed Shultz of the *Reading Eagle* (August 15, 1977) is classic. In his own words: "I couldn't sleep all week. I must have lost six or seven pounds worrying about this tournament. I like to be called the stopper and I like the team to depend on me. I knew the guys wanted to win the state tournament so they wouldn't have to play in the regional in Fox Hill, VA. This time of the year is what softball is about. The other games don't mean a thing if you don't make it to the national tournament. That is the goal of this team and I feel it is my job to get us there."

Discussing the tournament, he told Shultz, "Saturday night (in the 1-0 game against York) my fastball was really exploding. That was one of my best games of the year. This year I went back to pitching in the Allentown City League and I think it has made me a stronger pitcher. Today (Sunday) I threw a lot more drops and changeups. I had to use more changes of speed because I didn't get my fastball until about the sixth inning."

Santilli is philosophical about 1976, stating that familiarity with Allentown might have worked against his team's being able to show the necessary intensity against top-level opponents. He is also pleased that Delong, who missed the past national because of an injury, will be available. With the other teams learning what Jeff Seip can do, Zeke Delong, hitting behind him, becomes essential to their success.

On September 4th, the Sunners finish their regular season against Raybestos in a planned tune-up for both

Softball's Lefty Legend ~ Ty Stofflet

teams. Raybestos goes to Midland as the defending champ and Reading goes as the Pennsylvania State champ. The Sunners take four straight against the Cardinals for the second time this year.

Stofflet's record is 39-3 going into the national. Bergh is 26-2. The Sunners have regained their killer instinct, and they keep referring to this bad feeling that has stayed with them since last September. If they don't remember, the local newspapers have no problem reminding them that it's been 11 long months since they have been without a national crown. What do they intend to do about that?

In the 1977 national, Reading draws Raybestos and true to this year's form, they beat Al Lewis and the reigning champion Cardinals, 7-1. Raybestos takes a first-inning lead, but the Sunners get four in the fourth and three in the sixth. Seip and Gary Distasio hit home runs. This has been quite a favorable turn of events. Often when one team has dominated another throughout a season, anything can happen in a single game. This time the dominant team stays in the winners' bracket.

Bergh gets the next start and beats Mt. Eaton, 8-2. Larry gives up two runs on four hits, but his teammates register 13 hits, including home runs by Yoder and Seip. The Sunners have outscored their first two opponents, 15-2. Everybody understands, however, that this is not what championship softball is about, but merely the calm before the storm.

In the Sunners' third game, Ty draws Peterbilt of Seattle, with its Hall of Fame manager Tom Wagner. Throughout the years, Wagner is one of those players who hits Ty and this year is no exception. He is 2 for 3 with a triple and scores the only Seattle run after a sacrifice fly. Seattle manages just three hits. Art Weida brings in Seip

The Gang's All Here

and Yoder with a single in the top of the first to beat Graham Arnold (2-1). The Sunners have six hits, one by Stofflet.

Reading is back to grinding it out, but behind Ty's 13 strikeouts, they get their third tournament win. In his final at-bat, Wagner, with a runner on first, pops out to end the game. Arnold has eight strikeouts.

Billard's fourth game winds up to be one of the strangest games of the tournament. It is against Pontiac, Michigan's Edmore Johnson. It was Johnson, playing for Detroit in last year's national, who shut out the Sunners, to end their season.

The game started quietly enough with Barry Distasio and Bob Yoder opening the inning with base hits. Jeff Seip worked the count to 3-2 and took ball four. At that moment, Johnson charged the umpire, objecting to the call with profanity. He was thumbed out of the game and had to be escorted off the field by the police.

His replacement, Willie Gaffner, walked two of the next three batters, forcing home two runs. Later, Stofflet created a problem of his own, wild pitching a runner home from third to complete Pontiac's scoring.

In the fifth inning, Ty had another of those moments that he had been famous for. With two out and a runner on third, the ball hits Solarek's glove and bounces back toward the pitcher. Stofflet pounces on it, gets something on the throw to Carl, who holds it after getting knocked down by the runner.

At the conclusion of the game, Santilli specifically praises Solarek for his sparkling play. Ty has been somewhat erratic, but by now it is apparent that anything that interferes with the flow of a well-played game is very disturbing to him.

Softball's Lefty Legend ~ Ty Stofflet

Dave Kutch, covering for the *Reading Eagle*, interviewed Stofflet after the game (September 15, 1977). "After the ejection in the first inning, I couldn't concentrate. I guess I threw when I had to. I don't know. I just never got into it," he said.

Even though Stofflet is rattled, he only has hours to put himself together. The winners' final against Aurora is that night. Throughout his career, Stofflet has treated losses and teams that have beaten him as a personal challenge to his domain as reigning champ. Aurora has been one step from the best for the last few years and they are about as frustrated as a team can get. Even with Stofflet and Reading out of the running last year, they managed to lose to Raybestos. Expect short fuses all around. One thing for sure, Ty has chanted his private mantra, "Make them pay," whenever he has thought about this game. An added incentive is the matchup against Dick Brubaker, the other winning pitcher against them in last year's tournament.

The winners' bracket game is not close. The Sunners score one run in the third and another in the fourth. Brubaker narrows the score to 2-1 in the top of the sixth with a home run. The Sunners score three more runs in the bottom of the sixth to win, 5-1. Delong, Lalli and Weida have key hits.

The team has avenged last year's losses and turned the winners' final into a softball laugher. There is no doubt, however, that Ty is remembering Brubaker's home run and reminding himself for the next time they meet, "I carry a bat to the plate, too." There is nothing further to do but wait to see who climbs out of the losers' bracket.

Aurora manages to beat Seattle for the right to move on. Gary Hutchins pitches a shutout as Aurora wins, 2-0. The final will pit the Sunners against Home Savings, and

Ty, ASA Nationals - 1977

ASA Nationals - 1977

FIRST ROW: (Left to Right): James Steier, Robert Yoder, Barry Distasio, Joe Lalli, Gary Distasio, Richard DeLong.
SECOND ROW: Rocco Santilli, Manager; Paul Troika, Frank Orlando, Jeff Seip, Larry Thompson, Carl Solarek, Greg Radka.
THIRD ROW: Richard Goodman, Vice-President; Scott Keener, Art Weida, Larry Bergh, Rick Gruber, Ralph Kerschner, Coach; Ty Stofflet, John Steffy, Scorer; John Snyder, Coach; Abe Goodman, Chairman of the Board; Danny Goodman, Bat Boy; Michael Distasio, Bat Boy.
Missing from picture: John Erney, Denny Marchalonis.

1977 - ASA Champs

Softball's Lefty Legend ~ Ty Stofflet

most fans expect Stofflet against Brubaker, but both managers decide to use their second pitchers. To the softball purist, this is counted as a wasted opportunity, but there is reason behind Smith's and Santilli's decisions. Hutchins has a hot hand and Bergh has already won a game for Rocky in the tournament and has lost only one game all season.

Hutchins, however, shuts out the Sunners, while Bergh gives up three unearned runs as his team commits three errors. The final score is 3-0, and the two teams will play the "if" game.

In the last game against Stofflet, the Aurora manager, Smith, is unable to use Hutchins, who has developed a knot in his pitching arm. In fact, his only able-bodied pitcher for at the start of the game is the soon-to-be Hall of Fame pitcher, Harvey Sterkel.

Among Sterkel's claims to fame is a 19-strikeout performance in the national in 1959. At 43, Sterkel uses a slingshot delivery and a number of off-speed pitches to try to stave off the Sunners. But they get four runs on eight hits while Ty holds Aurora to three hits and no runs, 4-0. Carl Solarek has three RBI.

This is the victory that Ty describes as a "relief." Ever since the events of 1976, he has personally felt the pressure of getting back to the national and returning to the top rung of the nation's softball hierarchy. When the All-America choices are recorded, Stofflet is named MVP for his third tournament in four appearances. Art Weida joins him on the first team. Bob Yoder makes second team at third base.

Now that the Sunners have completed the season, they know what next year is expected to bring. As the national champions, they will be doing some traveling. If any rest is going to occur, it will have to be during the off-season.

The Gang's All Here Let's Have a Party

"I know one thing," says Ty. "This is a time I'd better be nice to Kathy and the girls. They have sure put up with a lot during the past few seasons."

If you remember back to June 6th, Ty lost his third game of the season to fall to 9-3. Since that date he has run off 35 consecutive wins, including five in the national. That means that during most of June, all of July and August and through the heart of September he has won every game he entered. Winter will give him time to review this accomplishment, but Ty does not ever want to look back. He expects that next year can be even better, and this time he may be right.

Hail the Conquering Heroes

YOU HAVE A PRETTY GOOD IDEA that your team has finally arrived when you start the calendar year with a reception for 750 adoring fans in the city of Reading. The Sunners receive proclamations from city, county and state officials. Congressman Gus Yatron presents a House resolution honoring the team for their contributions to amateur sports and for winning the 1977 U.S. Amateur Softball Association championship, and reads a letter of congratulations from President Jimmy Carter.

The Reading Municipal Stadium Commission presents rings and plaques to players, coaches and owners. Rocky thanks sponsor Abe Goodman of Billard Barbell and former sponsor John Kramer for their support of the team.

The team is now so popular that the event includes a "roast" of Rocky. A ton of good feelings is evident. There is a new set of numbers bandied about when discussing the prior year's team: 81-8, the won-lost record of the 1977 champions.

Something else has changed. Whereas Rocky had been politically correct in his assessment of his ace left-hander before the second national championship, he is now proclaiming that he and Reading have "the best pitcher in the world." It ain't bragging if it can be backed up, and the

Softball's Lefty Legend ~ Ty Stofflet

Sunners have backed Ty up with a 35-game winning streak. By now you have probably figured out that Ty expects the streak to continue.

Something in Ty's makeup covets adding another no-hit inning, another strikeout, another win or another championship to the previous one. Never will he say, "I've had too much success, it's time for me to let someone else take over." If you do beat him, you will have beaten whatever he had available to him that day. Don't rest, however, because the next time he faces you that internal chant, "Make them pay," will be demanding some form of restitution.

Between the lines he has become a legend of Paul Bunyonesque proportions. His pleasant demeanor prior to and after games makes the transformation to ferocious Tiger (as Rocky and the team called him) that much more intimidating. While on the mound he has only one focus – the batter's demise as quickly as possible.

Stofflet has opponents talking to each other in the following way: "When we faced (put in a current name) we knew we had a chance to get a hit. When we faced Ty, we knew we didn't have a chance."

Ronnie Kist made a particularly astute observation when he noted that Ty made most teams forget their game plan. "If we had bunters on the team who might have a chance to start something by putting the ball down against Ty, they tried to get a swinging hit because it would be on their resume for the rest of their life."

He noted that just seeing Ty on the sidelines made preparing for the game difficult. "And Ty had that stare that didn't invite comfort. If he knew that he was going to get you out, and you knew that he was going to get you out, then he was going to get you out."

Hail the Conquering Heroes

From the 1976, 20-inning game in Lower Hutt, New Zealand, to the Pennsylvania State Championship in 1977 to the ASA National, only Ty knew which pitches were working for him each game. But whatever it was, that became the recipe for shutting his opponent down. When all three pitches – riser, drop and changeup – are working, there is no chance for the other team to adjust, but he has become so adept at making do, that on days when only two of the three are available, only he and his catcher will know.

This is also a year for the Billard Sunners' manager, Rocky Santilli, to begin to gain some national ASA softball career recognition. Santilli has been selected an assistant coach for the 1979 USA Pan American team. Cliff Smith, his Aurora nemesis, will be head coach.

It is a long way from his starting point in Leesport, and he is happy to have been chosen for the post. "I really feel I was lucky to be selected," he tells the *Pennsylvania ASA Softball News* (July 1978). "I'm sure there were a lot of coaches under consideration." The article mentions that Santilli and the teams he has managed hold a combined record of 862 victories and 228 losses for a .781 winning percentage. It fails to note, however, that in recent years he has maintained that general winning percentage facing the best teams in the world.

Triumphant moments are all around. As predicted, the summer schedule now contains games played "by invitation only." That new category includes the National Sports Festival in Colorado Springs, CO, and a set of games in Victoria, British Columbia, and Yakima, WA, at the height of summer. The National Tournament will be back at Springfield, MO. This time you know that the locals will be aware that Reading is coming to town.

Softball's Lefty Legend ~ Ty Stofflet

At the beginning of the 1978 season, Ty is credited with 44 no-hitters and 17 perfect games. He was 5-0 in the last national with a 0.40 ERA. The team is approximately the same, except that Rocky has added Rich Rabin and Jody Koch in the outfield. Both are well known to Rocky, who plans to insert them in the starting lineup. Rabin has proved himself against the Sunners during the past year while playing for Worcester, MA. Now that Worcester has disbanded, Rocky has his pick of the team. Koch is a former Allentown Patriot ready to play against the best of the best.

If Rocky is experiencing one frustration, it is feeling that Larry Bergh has not quite demonstrated his full capabilities under top-flight competition. In the championship game that he lost, 3-0, against Aurora, to set up the "if" game, he made a mental error (throwing to the wrong base) that wound up being key to the outcome. Rocky would like to have that second "ace," but Larry is not quite there yet.

The season begins as a complete triumph, so that by the fourth of June, Billard is 17-1 with a team batting average of .364. Thirteen players are hitting above .300, led by Stofflet at a lofty .500. Ty continues to build up his consecutive-game win streak. He has not lost in over a year. As of July 3rd, Ty has 54 straight victories, and Rocky is using other pitchers and winning with little ball or by outslugging the competition.

This is the first year of softball's designated-hitter rule. The designated-hitter rule is familiar to anyone who follows American League baseball. Essentially, it is a way to take the pitcher out of the batting order and replace him with a hitter who does not play in the field.

This rule required some getting used to. Initially, pitch-

Hail the Conquering Heroes

ers were asked to hit only when their bat was needed in an expected tight game. Otherwise, the argument was, "we don't want you to get hurt." That allowed another player to feast off the deliveries of a lesser opponent, while the pitcher just sat on the bench between innings.

Now that the DH and its later partner, the re-entry rule, are well-established aspects of the game, it might seem silly to question what all the fuss was about. However, anyone who happens to be in the game at the moment any significant changes are initiated will describe the mental adjustments that occur in order to adapt to the new conditions.

Anyone who remembers the introduction of metal bats to both baseball and softball can try to tell your child what it was like to "saw the bat" out of a batter's hands with an inside pitch that struck the bat near the handle. Try the same thing with a metal bat and the result may be a pop fly over the infielders' heads.

When we watched Roger Clemens of the Yankees retrieve the broken bat of the Mets' Mike Piazza, then throw it in his direction in the World Series, it is hard to remember that broken bats aren't part of most people's playing experience. The wooden bat is, for most of us, part of the distant past.

The Billard Sunners are having an amazing summer run, and their ace continues to dominate in ways that defy comparison. On July 15th, he wins his 58th straight game against Da Ro's of Buchanon, NY. Twenty-four batters strike out in a 10-inning, 2-1 game. The only score comes when riseballs that Solarek can't reach allow a runner on first to advance.

The next stop is the National Sports Festival, where the top four U.S. teams – Billard Barbell, Santa Rosa , CA,

Softball's Lefty Legend ~ Ty Stofflet

Aurora, IL, and Seattle, WA – are featured in a two-games-against-each-team format.

The results are telling. Ty wins each of his scheduled games against these three teams and Bergh loses each of his. All teams end with 3-3 records so the finals selection was determined on run production. Santa Rosa and Billard make the final. Ty beats Santa Rosa, 3-0, with a two-hit, 12-strikeout performance.

He enters the tournament with a 61-game winning streak, faces the best teams in the U.S. and leaves with a 65-game winning streak. The mile-high air density has reduced the movement of his riseball to less than a foot, but he is now the consummate pitcher, taking whatever conditions come his way without complaint or concern, for he and his counterpart are on equal footing.

At this tournament, he describes to Ed Shultz of the *Reading Eagle* that he only has four working pitches available out of a repertoire of seven. "I didn't have my off-speed pitches. My drop kept me in there. My drop and my drop curve."

The artist is now at the height of his talents. He claims a pallet of seven pitches, but relies on four to compile a 4-0 festival record. An overpowering performance can now be accomplished with or without speed, depending on his majesty's preference. Sooner or later, he is bound to lose, but no one is quite sure what it will take.

That day finally comes during the road trip to Victoria, British Columbia, Yakima, WA, and Aurora, IL. Somewhat diluted because all players could not leave their jobs to make the trip, the team wound up with an 8-4 record. They swept the Canadians, won two of three against Washington and finished in Aurora, where they played four against Home Savings. It is in this series that

Hail the Conquering Heroes

Ty loses his first game in 72 contests. On Friday night, their first night in Aurora, Ty pitches a one-hit shutout and beats Dick Brubaker after Jeff Seip's 20th home run with a man on. On Saturday, Ty was pitching a shutout until he was tagged for six runs on five hits in the fifth.

Remember at all times when talking about Ty that the man is a purist. If you talk to him today about that streak, he will spend less time on the wins than on the defeat. "It was a long trip and a tiring one. I was not at my best that day, but we were scheduled for a two-day exhibition against Aurora and the crowd was there to see me pitch. It wasn't my way to disappoint them."

Ty tells the local newspaper (interview by Dave Lidecka), "Sooner or later it had to end. Hey, I'm only human. I just go out there and try to take them one at a time. I go out and try to do my best." The newspaper also quotes Barry Distasio, "You guys really did us a favor. It's (the win streak) been on his mind for the last 10 or 15 games. Now we can play ball."

Rocky noted that the team "just ran out of gas" by the time they played Aurora. But he also is aware that his team is better respected the farther they travel from home. During the trip he believes that they played before nearly 14,000 fans. It may have been a boost for Aurora, but in the end it probably will cost them more than they gained if they happen to meet Ty again in the national.

The club picks right up after the extended road trip and by the end of August, Ty has a new streak. Within a four-day period, he marks another milestone by throwing his 49th and 50th no-hitters. The 50th was one of those now-familiar Stofflet nights – 17 strikeouts, two walks and a fifth-inning, game-winning hit. Jeff Seip is again leading the team with a .404 batting average and Bob Yoder at

.402. Even in the age of the DH, Ty has 84 at-bats and is hitting a very respectable .345.

This is the year that Reading seems unable to do anything wrong. Their ace is nationally and internationally recognized as the premier pitcher in the game. Not just the best lefty, or the best hurler from the U.S., but the best in the game. His win streak was stopped at 36 for this year, and 71 for the combined 1977-78 seasons, but he is going to his fifth ASA national championship with a prior record of 14-5, including a five-game winning streak. His record for the 1978 season is 43-1.

The team exudes the kind of confidence that comes from experience gained throughout the country. Ty won all of his four National Sports Festival games, leading his team to the gold medal. The western swing was successful, with only Aurora putting a temporary damper on the festivities. And as Distasio said, it was good to get back to just playing ball rather than worrying about some improbable long streak.

The 1978 ASA National Major Fast Pitch Tournament is held in Springfield, MO, a place with which the Sunners are quite familiar. It was here seven years ago that they were crowned Cinderella team of the tournament and finished fourth. At that time, it might have been possible to sneak up on an opponent or two. This year they come in as defending champs, having won two of the last three years.

Dave Kutch of the *Reading Eagle* filed a story (September 9, 1978) to which all quotes about a game against Clear Lake are attributed. Ty opens the tournament with a no-hitter against the team that had hit 101 homers during their regular season. Rocky Santilli is understated in the 5-0 Sunner victory. "Ty was throwing loosely tonight," he said. "He's been good all year, but threw very easy tonight. That's when the ball moves best, when he's not overthrowing – just like on the sidelines. I don't think that team is used to that caliber of pitching. I'm sure they were quite impressed."

Carl Solarek's reaction was also captured. "The more I catch Ty, the more I realize what a superstar he is," said Solarek. "He had everything tonight: his fastball was super, his drop was busting at the plate, he had a super rise and exceptional change. He got stronger as the game progressed."

Ty's reaction was vintage. "The national tournament is special," said Stofflet. "You see your friends and it's like a world championship event. It would be super to win here. The 1971 tournament here was the first for the team, so it would be great to win here."

Littleton, CO, is the next opponent and they are dispatched quickly. Larry Bergh pitches a one-hitter, striking out 17. Reading gets 11 hits, including a Solarek home run, to win, 5-0.

The third game is against Raybestos, and Ty is back on the mound. The matchup is Stofflet-Lewis, and as the saying goes, these two teams do not like each other. They normally play eight or more games against one another during the season, and the spot in the national tournament that they both covet is at the top of the heap. There is nothing to tell the Sunners about Al Lewis or the Cardinals about Ty Stofflet that they don't already know.

Jeff Seip has been somewhat quiet with the bat through the first two games. His two RBI have come with sacrifice flies. He is pressing and he knows it. "The wind was really blowing in from center field that game. Some people thought that there was no way to hit one out of the park. I decided to swing nice and easy, and wouldn't you know it, I get two that go right through the teeth of the gale, into the center field bleachers.

The Sunners win, 4-0, on a one-hit, 14-strikeout effort by Stofflet and Seip's two home runs. In the sixth inning, with the count 3-0 on Seip, Santilli gave the hit sign. His reasoning, as told to Dave Kutch (September 12, 1978), "I knew Lewis was too proud to walk Jeff. I figured he'd come in with the pitch, so I gave the hit sign." And there went the second home run.

This has been a surprising day in the tournament. The Sunners next will face San Antonio, TX, on the strength of their wins over Aurora, IL, 1-0, and Santa Rosa, CA, 1-0. Aurora is also on their way home today because York, PA, beat them, 2-1. Their four-year, second-place streak has ended.

The pitcher behind San Antonio's success in this tournament is David Scott, who is on his way to a distinguished career. In the winners' bracket final, Scott and Stofflet get locked into a 1-1 game through the first six innings. The crowd is buzzing about a tape measure shot hit off Ty by left fielder Art Washington. It is the only San Antonio hit to this point, but it has tied the game.

In the top of the seventh, Reading scores two runs. A Solarek single, a Rabin triple and a Yoder squeeze bunt account for the scoring. Ty has 16 strikeouts and no walks in a 3-1 victory. Scott throws a five-hit, six-strikeout, five-walk effort in the loss. Rocky's plan is working like a charm. His new players are contributing, while the "old reliables" find new ways to be counted on.

The winners' bracket final against Springfield ends up a 6-1 "laugher" in eight innings, but nobody on the Sunners was even smiling in the bottom of the Springfield seventh. It is the matchup that the crowd has been waiting

Hail the Conquering Heroes

to see: Ty Stofflet vs. Roy Burlison. The game starts out with an oddity, Yoder doubling and scoring after two wild pitches in the first. In the fifth, however, a Ted Hicks single and a Steve Hutchinson triple tie the score.

In the seventh, after misplaying a single into a double, Rabin makes a redeeming running catch in right center to extend the game. In the eighth, Stofflet pulls a Burlison pitch near the right field line for a triple. Rabin gets an opposite field single to push his team ahead for good. After a stolen base and an error, Burlison leaves the game. The Sunners score five and win going away.

Ty's reactions to Kutch (September 15, 1978) now include thoughts about his hitting and his pitching, and no pitcher who ever played games this important has a problem talking about his hitting. "I was guessing right on a rise," said Stofflet about his triple. "Burlison popped a good one and I had the bat at the right place."

Regarding his pitching, "I had my speed, but made a mistake on the 0-2 pitch to Hutchinson. I tried to throw him a waste pitch, but it flattened out. I should have shut them out, but the important thing is that I look at the scoreboard and see that we have six runs and they have only one. I don't care if I gave up 10 hits, as long as we win."

The Sunners are now sitting pretty, waiting to see whether Santa Rosa, CA (82-20), Clearwater, FL (85-16), or Springfield, MO (73-25), will play them in the final. In the end, Clearwater beats Santa Rosa and Springfield to reach the finals.

Earlier I mentioned the egos necessary to pitch and hit top-caliber softball. I left out the ego required to build an international power from scratch when doubters can be found in all directions. Rocky Santilli will acknowledge

Softball's Lefty Legend ~ Ty Stofflet

that the greatest pitcher of his era is his pitcher. No one knows more than he does the confidence derived from sending No. 18 to the mound. But he has not assembled a one-man wrecking crew. He has surrounded his ace with an extremely talented supporting cast, and he aims to show the world that his team can win a championship game with Stofflet on the sidelines.

By this time, he is aware that Larry Bergh is an extremely talented pitcher who works in Ty's shadow. Bergh had a chance to win the championship game the previous year, but misplays and Larry's mental error of not throwing to the right base did not get the job done. He would like to change matters this year, and once again has the luxury of the winners' bracket perspective to accomplish that change. Clearwater will have to beat him twice in order to take home the championship.

Dave Kutch again is our eyes and ears on the field (September 17, 1978), as he recounts the events for the *Reading Eagle*. The game starts as a seesaw encounter with Reading ahead, 2-1, in the Clearwater half of the fifth. The key play of the game proves that Clearwater had scouted Larry and wanted to test him.

With Stofflet warming up and Leon Wood on first base, Wood attempts a delayed steal of second. A delayed steal is meant to surprise the opposing team and rattle the pitcher into throwing the ball wildly. Instead, Bergh narrowly makes the play to second for the second out. In the bottom of that inning, the Sunners put five runs on the board to move ahead, 7-1. The final score is 9-2. Bergh is more relieved that exultant. "Early, I was having trouble with my drop," he tells Kutch. "So I went to my change-up. They were having trouble with the change and I had a good riseball. But it seemed every inning they had some-

Hail the Conquering Heroes

thing going. I'm just glad I was able to finish the game." Bergh has given up nine hits, but he has nine strikeouts, and he has triumphed.

Stofflet told Kutch, "I think I was more concerned with Larry than I was with the championship. I really wanted him to win this game." Santilli added, "I think we proved again that we are a team. Everybody keeps saying we only have Stofflet. I say we have a pretty good team."

To underscore Rocky's remarks, five Sunners are selected to the ASA All-America first team – Stofflet, Solarek, Seip, Yoder and Delong. Bergh is a second-team selection. Ty is selected co-MVP along with Ted Hicks, who has broken the record for most hits in the tournament with 12 and finishes with a record batting average of .632.

Billard finishes the season 75-13. They have posted a two-season record of 156-21 and have triumphed in three of the last four nationals. When you add the 1976 ISF tri-championship in New Zealand, their record stands at four championships in four years. There is every reason to be optimistic. This year, six players received All-America recognition and the final game was won without needing their ace. It's good to be the king of softball.

How Do You Spell Dynasty?

THE FIRST INKLING THAT YOU might get that changes will mark the 1979 Reading team is that Bob Hoffman of York Barbell has taken over the sponsorship of the team. "Mr. Softball," as he is known in Pennsylvania, will sponsor 16 teams this year, including two in fast pitch. While both will be named York, they will be completely separate.

The move from a Berks County to a York sponsor may not seem significant to an outsider, but this represents a major and unwanted move to those in Reading who have called the Sunners their team. Now that the local juggernaut has attained top-dog status, no Berks sponsor or combination of sponsors will come forward and be an "angel" for the four-time champs. Articles appear in both the news and editorial sections of the *Reading Eagle* bemoaning the plight of the team. The writers understand why it must be done. They don't approve of their county's collective stinginess.

Rocky explains that Billard had saved the club three years ago but was unable to increase the budget that a national traveling team requires to meet scheduling obligations. Among the team's trips will be those to another National Sports Festival and to exhibitions in Aurora, IL, Minot, ND, San Antonio, TX, and the ASA national in Midland, MI.

Softball's Lefty Legend ~ Ty Stofflet

There are additional issues for the team. Five players, Stofflet, Seip, Gary Distasio, second baseman Rick Gruber and Rich Rabin will be trying out for the Pan American team in Colorado Springs, CO. Zeke Delong, Bob Yoder, Larry Bergh and Carl Solarek are declared ineligible because each has played a professional sport.

Trials begin May 29 and last for 10 days. The U.S. Pan Am softball team is the first of its kind, with 18 players being selected from among 60 of the nation's best. After the selections, the team will play exhibitions in the U.S., followed by the Games, which will be held in San Juan, Puerto Rico, July 1-15.

The April 28, 1979, headline in the *Eagle* sums up the situation quite nicely, "Barbells Face Year of Distractions." John Snyder will sub as manager and such players as Joe Lalli, who sat out the past season with an injury, will fill in. It is makeshift all around. Bob Yoder has finally retired, however, after leading the team with a .416 batting average. A bat that good will always be missed.

The odd season moves along as Stofflet, Seip and Gruber are named to the Pan Am team. Other pitchers selected include Al Lewis, David Scott and Gene Green of Maryland. By this time, Ty Stofflet is the man who generates newsprint superlatives wherever he goes. When interviewed during this phase of his career, however, he is much less interested in talking about himself, than in trying to do something that will reverse the decline his sport is experiencing.

One hope that he and his teammates have is that an international-game format will eventually lead to Olympics competition. If that occurs, fast pitch softball will generate much more interest worldwide. Until such time, however, he is left to watch the term "softball"

How Do You Spell Dynasty?

become synonymous with the slow pitch game. The purist in him finds that trend appalling.

One of the U.S. team's problems is described by *United Press International* (*Reading Eagle*, July 3, 1979). According to the story, the specter of facing the U.S. All-Stars has caused three international teams – Cuba, Argentina and Mexico – to drop out of the competition. Stofflet's 1978 record of 42-1 and his 104.7 mph clocking are prominently featured in the article. His lone loss is described as his seventh game in six days, to explain why perfection was not to be his that day.

In the Pan Am Games, Ty pitches a three-hit shutout against Canada, 3-0. He is described as the "crown prince in the world of softball pitchers" who can beat the opposition with any part of his dazzling assortment. In the *UPI* article, he engages in a bit of gamesmanship against the Canadians, as he says," I didn't throw as hard as I normally do. They have faced me twice before and they knew what to expect, so I changed speeds on them."

He goes on, "I had to mix it up. Otherwise, they would just stick the bat out there and hit the ball to the opposite field. I barely threw the ball 85 mph, but the next time I pitch I'll throw 100 mph. I guarantee it."

If you were the Canadian team at that time reading the newspaper account, you could expect to be put somewhat off your game. Here, the other pitcher has announced that today's pitching colors are somewhat subdued, but he intends to go back to "dead red" the next time he faces you. It's bad enough that you have to anticipate a 100 mph pitch. As Jim Brackin noted earlier, the added possibility of something a lot slower brings it to a guessing game that favors the guy on the mound.

The championship Pan Am Game again pits Stofflet

Softball's Lefty Legend ~ Ty Stofflet

and the U.S. against Canada. The Pan Am format is similar to that of the Olympics format. Losses in earlier rounds are not counted in championship rounds, therefore, although Canada has two losses and the U.S. has none, this is a winner-take-all game. Rob Guenter is the Canadian pitcher.

As one would expect, the game is another "hitless wonders" affair. After 13 innings, the score is 0-0. In the 14th, Canada pushes across a run with a walk, single and groundout. Years later, even in the comfort of his recreation room, Santilli continues to be bothered by that loss, because he believes that his teammate, Jeff Seip, would have been a terrific asset to the U.S. team if he had been used more. As it was, Seip went 4 for 6 in the tournament.

Upon returning home, Ty shows this old adage, "make the next one pay," as he throws a perfect game to start the Reading Invitational Softball Tournament. Stofflet acknowledges that it will take time to get over that loss, but the team in front of him, County Fuels of Baltimore, has helped him reconnect with the Sunners once again. It is time to regain his focus on York Barbell softball.

What's in a name, you might ask, as we move from label to label to describe the Sunners-Billard-York softball team? To the sponsor, it is the reason the investment is made and the justification for the expenditure. To the long-time fan, however, it is a temporary way to keep track of the team in the local newspapers. The Sunners-Billard-York franchise will be wearing York uniforms this year, but if Rocky is standing in the dugout, then it is acceptable to think of them as the Sunners.

The national is held in Midland, MI, and the Reading team is set to face Guanella Brothers of Santa Rosa, CA, the same team that has gone to the National Sports

How Do You Spell Dynasty?

Festival. It features Chuck D'Arcy as its ace. Guanella is able to muster a single and a hit batter in the fifth inning, but a Stofflet strikeout ends the inning. In the bottom of the fifth, after a couple of hits, Solarek hits a bullet (scored an error) that accounts for the only run of the game. Stofflet strikes out eight.

The next day they face Raybestos. Wildness by a combination of Raybestos pitchers results in two first-inning runs. Ty had first-inning problems, too, giving up two hits and two walks, enabling the Cardinals to score once. However, York Barbell scores twice in the second on a single by Delong with the bases loaded, and Ty does not allow a hit the rest of the way as Reading wins, 4-1.

In his interview with H. J. Deitz, *Eagle* sports writer (September 9, 1979), Ty explains his first-inning control problems as well as his strategy for adjustment. "There was a light ball and a heavy ball. The light ball kept taking off and I couldn't bring it down. It's tough to adjust. Out here (in the national) it's altogether different. You've got to adjust quicker. There's no room for mistakes."

So Stofflet threw risers with the light ball and drops with the heavy ball. When the umpire throws out a lemon, it's time to make lemonade. Zeke Delong again demonstrates why it's so important to have someone in the batting order who can respond when the other team walks Seip. His two-run single provides for a comfortable game against a tough foe.

The third game, against Wilson-Powell of Washington, D.C., pits two regional rivals against one another in a national contest. Ty is selected because Bergh has already faced this team three times this year. Ty once again proves that he can be a different pitcher any night of the week. Up to this point he has been relying on drops

'79 ASA Yearbook

How Do You Spell Dynasty?

and changeups but tonight it's time for Wilson-Powell to face the heater. It must have been a hot night because he throws a one-hit shutout, striking out 15. Bergh is scheduled to throw against Phoenix, AZ.

The score is 1-0, Reading, after four innings, but Bergh gets in trouble in the fifth and after Phoenix ties the score, Ty is brought in. His relief role is just what the manager ordered and York Barbell wins, 3-1, in eight innings. Everything up to now is going according to form, except that this is a team that is not hitting, and Rocky is making lineup changes to take advantage of team speed. The team continues to win, but this year is not feeling like 1978.

In the final of the winners' bracket, Reading faces McArdle Pontiac of Midland, MI, whose ace is Owen "The Fog" Walford. He is called The Fog for obvious reasons – nobody sees the ball too well when he is at his best. In the top of the seventh, York scores its first run on a Seip home run. The bottom of the seventh sees a Stofflet wild pitch strikeout result in a runner on first, which is followed by a bunt hit over the incoming third baseman's head for runners on first and second with no out. A sacrifice and a wild pitch lead to the Michigan tally.

Six innings later, Rabin loops a single to left that scores Lalli with the go-ahead run. Two more runs in that inning make the final score 4-1, but it has been anything but easy. At the game's end, Terry Collins, the McArdle manager, has these comments regarding Ty.

"We just did not move the ball like I thought we were capable of moving the ball against him (Stofflet). We stayed with them. He's tough. He doesn't get the name, the reputation, he doesn't get as far as he has if he isn't tough." Collins finishes with a challenge to his players, "If the guys have enough heart and enough guts so they want to come

Softball's Lefty Legend ~ Ty Stofflet

back here Saturday night, then we'll win tomorrow night."

The victory in extra-innings is Ty's 14th consecutive in this tournament. He strikes out 19 and now possesses a five-game tournament winning streak. Santilli expresses praise for the new young gun, Walford, but rides his own Tiger to the tournament finale.

Collins gets his wish as Bob Ryan, who scattered seven hits, pitches Midland to a 2-0 win over Santa Rosa. The stage is set for a Walford-Stofflet rematch. This time it is Walford, however, who throws eight innings of no-hit ball as the game remains scoreless. In the ninth, York loads the bases but fails to score and in the 10th, a hit batsman, a single to left and a sac fly beat Ty and Reading, 1-0.

Why did Rocky go out of his usual order and throw Ty first, you might ask? Or what do you do now that your ace has lost the first game in extra innings? These are questions that can be posed for the next 100 years, but the result will still be the same. In the "if" game, Rocky sits Ty down and throws Larry.

Newspaper reports consistently indicate that the highly partisan crowd of more than 9,500 made it difficult for players to hear one another. But it is my guess that Midland was elated when the best pitcher in the world was on the sidelines for this game.

Ryan goes back to the mound for Midland and Bergh is the Reading pitcher. For three innings the game is scoreless, but in the fourth, a double by this year's MVP, Jeff Peck, followed by a single and a passed ball provide Midland with their first run. In the next inning, Rod Johnson plays ultimate "little ball" with a single, two stolen bases and a throwing error. Another run in the sixth closes out the scoring for Midland in a 3-1 win.

In a stunning, three-hour period, the dynasty has taken a

How Do You Spell Dynasty?

big hit. Only Scott Keener in the outfield and Stofflet are named first team All-Americans. Seip gets a second-team nod. Both Midland pitchers, Walford and Ryan, share first-team pitching honors with Ty. The York team finishes 5-2 for second place. Reading breaks two national records this year. Ty has the new mark for consecutive wins by a pitcher at 14; York ties the Clearwater Bombers for most consecutive team wins at 12.

At the conclusion of the tournament, everyone said the right thing about winning as a team and losing as a team, but this is a shocking defeat that is only matched by the double loss to Virginia in 1973 which kept them from getting to the national. Ty immediately makes it clear, however, that he will be rejoining the team for the next season and Rocky is even more determined to get more players to help the ball club.

Something in the description of the recent national that might have been missed deserves mention. Two pitchers, Graham Arnold of Peterbilt in Seattle and Owen Walford of McCardle Pontiac in Midland, MI, have come from New Zealand to play ball. Teams have had a national character for many years, but now they have achieved an international element as well. Talent from all over the globe is coming to play in the U.S. during the five months of summer ball in the Northern Hemisphere.

Rocky's idea of getting a ballplayer from some exotic place extends to New Jersey, Maryland or Virginia. He is struggling to keep his tournament-caliber team together, while trying to compete with owners who can provide jobs with a decent salary for their players. He is excited about David Scott, a Pennsylvania native, joining his team after time in service. Otherwise, nothing on the horizon signals a big difference to the makeup of his club for next year.

Coping with Change

What a Difference a Moment Makes

IT COULD HAPPEN TO ANY OF US at any time, but we usually don't give it a thought. Ty to this day does not want to talk about it, but sometime in January, 1980, he injured his pitching wrist while at work. At first, the prognosis was positive. He would be able to get back before the major tournaments. But Stofflet may have tried to push things along by getting out of his cast prematurely.

Whatever the story, during the 1980 season he has had to endure two separate casts and the wrist has been in considerable pain throughout each of his attempted rehabs. There is no other conclusion to be reached, but that the Sunners will have to get along as best they can without him.

Reading makes it to the national again, and it brings Larry Bergh and 44-year-old George Ulmer as the complete pitching staff, as the word around the ball fields is that the king will be sitting out these games. The Tiger has been put in a plaster of Paris cast.

Throughout the year of inactivity, Ty is a man without a place to be comfortable. Going to the ballpark does nothing for his general well-being. In fact, it makes him downright upset as person after person ask him the same questions. How are you? When do you think it will heal? And the not so subtle, do you think that you'll ever throw that fast again?

Softball's Lefty Legend ~ Ty Stofflet

At the time of the injury he is 38, but he won't be getting back to playing until the summer when he turns 40. He speaks confidently to the media but there is a look in his eyes that says, "This is an awful place for me to be, so close and yet so far from the national stage."

Carl Solarek, his catcher for the past seven years, is a veteran of both softball and hardball wars. He likens going to the national as getting together with friends from throughout the country who deserve recognition as the top tier of fast pitch. "Every year you who get reacquainted with the guys. It was like homecoming. All the best teams and the top players knew and respected one another."

This year, Reading has added Don Van Deusen, a shortstop-second baseman from Virginia. He is an all-tools player whom teammates call the smoothest they've ever seen at short. Seip is struck by the irony of getting Van Deusen at the same time the team loses Stofflet. "Here are two beacons, who we hoped would be playing together. Instead, Donny comes to the team and Ty has to sit out the year."

Larry Bergh gets his first chance to be the ace at a national tournament, but the debut is not a success. In the first game against Lakewood, CA, Reading scores three runs to lead. But in the fifth and sixth, California counters with five and the Pennsylvanians are sent to the losers' bracket, 5-3.

In the second game, Bergh bounces back with a two-hit shutout against Baltimore. Van Deusen goes 3 for 3 with an RBI after going 2 for 4 in the first game. In the third game, Seip and Koch hit home runs as Ulmer beats Winston-Salem, 9-4. The next game, however, is the tournament shocker, because Bergh was leading by three runs needing one more out in the bottom of the seventh when

What a Difference a Moment Makes

Bob Sagle, playing for ADM, guessed "changeup" and hit a three-run home run to tie the game. George Ulmer finished the game for Reading, which loses in the ninth on another three-run inning.

In the *Eagle* sports section's lead story on September 11, 1980, Rocky is frank in his assessment of the team's performance. "We hit, but we just didn't get the pitching when we needed it. Larry just didn't pitch the way he is capable of pitching. You can't blow leads in the seventh and expect to stick around."

It has been an extremely frustrating season, concluding with the team uncharacteristically scoring three or more runs in games that they lost. Rocky's attempt to boost Larry Bergh to the top spot on the team has not worked, and no one is sure just how well the man with the cast on his wrist will fare once crunch time returns next year.

The Return of the Tiger

THE ARTICLES THAT APPEARED throughout Ty's absence from the softball wars quote fans and players alike who speak as though they have lost something quite special. Even the players in the City League who got to flail away during his weekday workouts express sadness at not being able to see softball perfection in their backyard.

He has become an accessible treasure, able to be taken for granted because of his durability. For 20 years, he has never had an injury that kept him off the field for any extended time. Even his spiked hand in the 1974 national didn't prevent him from winning the MVP for his pitching and hitting after the incident.

He is unprepared for the injury, and that is partly why he tries to get back too soon. But having broken the wrist bone that takes the longest to heal, he finally decides to take what Mother Nature has dished out and wait for the next season.

In the June 13, 1981 *Allentown Morning Call*, Dan Shope interviews Ty about his prospects for the new season. Ty admits that he should have left his cast on for three months but with the season starting he wanted to force his recovery.

There is also a new reality with which to cope. His days of 100 mph fastballs may be a part of his past. He will

Softball's Lefty Legend ~ Ty Stofflet

continue to have guile and an assortment of pitches that make him dangerous any time he pitches, but after 20 years, the uncanny heater may be just a little less intimidating. He has only one loss until now and on June 6, 1981, sports an 11-1 record, but he speaks of things that have previously been foreign to him, such as a sore back. Getting back into the game at his top level will be a struggle.

But then again, when summer returns and the spring chill is removed from evening games, players can move around just a little bit easier. Playing for the renamed Reading Sunners, Ty throws an 18-inning game against Solomon's of New Jersey and pitches a vintage 33-strikeout, 1-0 victory. Ty is obviously pleased and begins thinking of the task ahead, getting ready for the 1981 national.

It is at this point that the vagaries of softball sponsorship again merit almost as much attention in the news as the prospective lineup. York has pulled out as sponsor and a group of Reading businesses have pooled their resources to back the team. Ty goes into this year's national with a 36-6 record, three no-hitters, 536 strikeouts in 325 innings and an ERA of 0.68.

The *Reading Eagle* has sent Harry Deitz, Jr. to cover the national. His articles appear September 10-19, 1981. All quotations that follow are taken from his reports.

Rocky Santilli is confident but tentative. His starting lineup now showcases Don Van Deusen and Jeff Seip along with Ty. Seip has once again led the team in hitting (.348 average, 24 home runs, 71 RBI) and is as feared a hitter as any currently playing. Van Deusen has hit .326 with a team-leading 87 hits. Steve Moore (third base), Joe Lalli (second base) and Carl Solarek (catcher) complete the

The Return of the Tiger

infield. Zeke Delong, Jody Koch, Terry Kreider and Scott Keener will play the outfield and DH if necessary.

Reading has a 15-game winning streak going into the national and has had a relatively easy draw. They get a first-round bye and will not start their first game until some teams have completed their second. The 1981 overall record of 71-21 compares favorably with that of the stronger years in the '70s. Rocky notes, however, that overall team speed is not what it used to be. "This team's a little slower, but overall it might hit a shade better. Unless we're facing another of the top pitchers in the country, even if Ty is off a little, we're hoping we can still win."

Stofflet (September 11) puts his own spin on the layoff of a full year. "I feel that the year off helped me. I don't get tired." He answers questions about endurance and speed with the confidence that he has demonstrated throughout his career. Being at the national with opening day in sight is no time to let any negativity cramp his style.

Rocky is also upbeat about his flamethrowing left-hander. He claims not to see much difference between Ty's 1981 fastball and that of the '70s. "There's only one pitch I didn't see him get back and that was the straight change. And I don't think he needs that." Deitz adds to the evidence of Ty's complete return by pointing to his attitude. He cites Ty's readiness. "I think I'm ready, and I think we'll do well. I think we'll win this thing. I've got a feeling."

The September 13 installment of the *Eagle's* national coverage takes as its focus the life of a softball family, with a half-page photograph of Ty and Kathy Stofflet near a ball field. Kathy offers advice to softball wives. "I would say go to the games. Be there and enjoy the games as they do. That makes a difference."

When asked about the year off from softball, Kathy

Softball's Lefty Legend ~ Ty Stofflet

says, "It was a slow summer. This is our way of life. For nine years we traveled. Last year was boring." Kathy goes on to say that she has watched Ty play softball for 21 years, the last 18 as wife to her record-setting husband. It is a life that suits this family quite well.

With the preliminaries over, it is time to play ball. The Sunners draw West Liberty, OH, and Jeff Seip turns the game into his own private fireworks display. In three at-bats he hits a run-producing triple and two solo home runs. Ty is a bit rusty, but manages to hang around for seven innings and wins, 7-3. The crowd has seen a win, but not an overpowering effort. His comments? "When I got a couple of runs I took it easy. I wasn't bustin' as much and I wasn't sharp. I felt good when I went out there, but the ball wasn't zipping."

At this moment, Stofflet's record in the nationals is 29-6, with victories in 15 of the last 16 games. The first run allowed broke a 38-inning string of no earned runs allowed. Cedar Rapids is next.

The headlines (September 15) read, "Ty Fires 25th Perfect Game" and "Stofflet Pulls Page Out of History." And one gets the sense that all of Reading can take a breath. The King has come back to claim his throne. This is Ty's second perfect game in Missouri, 10 years apart, and he is now a senior statesman for his sport. The final score is 2-0. Five different players contribute to the scoring.

"I had everything, change, hard drop and riseball. Maybe it was my night for one," says Ty. In comparing his perfect games, he is quick to respond. "This one I like the best because I'm coming off a year with the injury. I never thought I would get to throw again in a national tournament. It makes me feel good up here."

He added, "People who were out here Sunday night

figured I didn't have it anymore. People thought I was washed up." He commented further, "But I wanted people to know that it's me out there. That was me tonight (in the perfect game). I wanted people to know I'm back. I'm really back."

Against Cedar Rapids, Solarek identified the hard drop as Stofflet's best pitch. The next opponent is Ashland, OH, and it is the same pitch that betrays Ty. "He didn't have the drop, Solarek says. "It was hard and straight. He had it, but it wasn't moving (September 15)."

Hank Miller, the Ashland pitcher, makes no bones of his strategy. In a nutshell, stay away from Seip. "They have other great hitters in the lineup, but he'll kill you. He hit one against me in '77 that went 400 feet."

Ashland scored a run in the first and two more on a home run by Jim Messner. The Sunners never get into it as they are shut out, 3-0. Stofflet has seen his team against junkballers before and knows that they always seem to give the team fits. But in the end he concludes, "We just weren't up for it."

The next game is against Guanella Brothers of Santa Rosa, CA (September 18), and Ty is back to his winning ways. He strikes out 14 while scattering six hits to win in 10 innings, 3-0. Steve Moore, who is having an All-American tournament, hits a three-run, walk-off home run for Reading.

"I was strong tonight," said Stofflet. "I was popping the ball real good tonight. The more I throw, the better I get." He also allows that by not shutting out Ashland, the burden for the loss is his. "That's my job and I didn't do that last night."

In his next game of the tournament, Ty faces St. Joseph, the home team, and wins, 2-1, on a two-hitter.

Softball's Lefty Legend ~ Ty Stofflet

Van Deusen steals a run in the first by scoring from second on an infield hit. In the fifth a Lalli triple followed by a Krause single puts Reading ahead for good. Ty strikes out 11, getting stronger as the game progresses.

The Sunners lose their second game with Bergh on the mound vs. Ashland again, 3-2. Bergh was in trouble throughout his 2 1/3 innings and was relieved by Stofflet after walking in a run. Ty strikes out 11 in less than five innings but lets in two runs in the third. Reading scores single runs in the fifth and sixth, but the damage is done and the team has to settle for third place in the tournament.

This means that Reading, St. Joseph, Decatur and Ashland will compete in the 1982 National Sports Festival. It is a consolation prize, to be sure, but one that recognizes that Reading is back with Ty as their ace as a national softball power. The team ends the season 75-23. Ty's complete season record is 40-7. As of the end of the 1981 season, his record in the nationals is 32-7, an .821 winning percentage.

Getting Back to Championship Form?

THE 1982 SUNNERS ARE NOW the Bank of Pennsylvania Sunners and their record coming into the 1982 national is 55-29. It has been three years since they have sat atop the perch of reigning champion, and they are no longer one of the favorites entering the Midland, MI, national tournament.

The summer has been one of preparation and practice for the Sunners. At 55-29, they are not nearly the juggernaut of prior years, but when Ty goes to the mound, as the saying goes, anything can happen.

This year, a new tiebreaker rule has been added to reduce the number of extended, extra-inning games. After seven innings, every half-inning will start with a runner on second and no out. In the highlight set of games for the Sunners' summer, Reading makes it to the National Sports Festival championship game. Decatur and Reading are tied, 4-4, after seven innings. In the top of the 10th inning, Reading fails to score on an interference call. In the bottom of the inning, Decatur succeeds for a 5-4 victory over Stofflet.

The rest of the season progresses as expected, with enough games to make sure that Ty and his teammates

Softball's Lefty Legend ~ Ty Stofflet

will be fresh for the only part of the year that truly matters, the national championship.

The Sunners draw Guanella Brothers of Santa Rosa and have a fortunate beginning. In the top of the first Peter Brown allows two Sunner runs on wild pitches. In the fourth, Stofflet gives up three singles for the first Guanella run. A Sunner error ties the score. It remains that way until the eighth when Ray Allena hits a home run off Stofflet for the win. Final score, 3-2, Santa Rosa.

Stofflet comes back with a one-hit shutout to beat Portland, ME. The win makes him 29-10 for the year, and keeps the Sunners in the tournament. Rocky would like to use Bergh next, but he has a sore wrist and is unable to go. Stofflet is the replacement.

The game against Lakewood, CA, is played in a drizzle, which befits its outcome. Ty has a perfect game through six innings. The game goes nine innings and Ty loses on a dropped fly ball in the outfield with runners on, 1-0. In the rain, nothing is routine. Ty strikes out seven. He ends the year 29-11.

For Rocky, the 1982 Sunners team was definitely a step backward. He has done his homework over the winter and the 1983 has a new look. The main changes are a soon-to-be-Hall-of-Fame shortstop, Jim Brackin, and a new pitcher, Rod Jarvis, to replace Lalli, Bergh, Delong, Solarek and Gary Distasio. This is the 13th year of reporting team changes and one thing remains constant. As long as No.18 has the ball, and something important is on the line, anything can happen.

The 1983 Sunners take an early trip to Clearwater, FL, to meet the Bombers, and take advantage of the heat in early May. Ty chooses this opportunity to put all oppo-

Getting Back to Championship Form?

nents on notice, by throwing a no-hitter (3-0), followed by a one-hitter (2-0 in 10 innings). In 44 years, this is only the fourth no-hit game thrown against Clearwater.

Later this spring, Stofflet leads Reading into the Memorial Day Lancaster Tournament. After round-robin play against the six other tournament teams, the Sunners (5-2) and Linden (N.J.) Merchants (6-1) hook up in the final. Ty beats Richie Hoppe. Key hits come from Seip (home run) and Van Deusen (two-run double). With relief help from Jarvis, Ty is also the tournament MVP. In his first 12 games, Stofflet is 10-2 with 126 strikeouts in 77 innings and an ERA of 0.38.

The Sunners and their ace are once again sounding optimistic. While it is acknowledged that Ty can no longer pitch the same load as he has in the past, he has added more exercise to his winter regimen, including weight training, to make his arm stronger. Most important, he has lost about 15 pounds and seems to have regained his stamina.

Once again Ty is selected to try out for the USA Pan American team. The tryouts are held at Colorado Springs, CO, again, and Ty has the best record among all pitchers. He is pleased to attend the Games, which will be held in Caracas, Venezuela, but at 42, he wants to make this trip his last. Dave Scott, Vaughn Alvey and Chuck D'Arcy complete the pitching roster.

The Sunners take a successful tour through Canada late that summer, with visits to Regina, Saskatchewan and Winnipeg. However, while they go 6-0 on the trip, Ty pulls a muscle in Winnipeg and has to be relieved. He misses two weeks, returning for the national qualifier in August, when he beats Allentown, 2-1. Jarvis also wins, 2-1, to complete the sweep and clinch the qualification.

Softball's Lefty Legend ~ Ty Stofflet

In the Pan Am Games, Ty wins his two starts. His first, against the Virgin Islands, is a 14-2 blowout. The second against the Dominican Republic, is a good, old-fashioned 3-2 softball game, with the U.S. winning in eight. Butch Batt, the oldest player for the U.S., gets the winning hit for Stofflet, the second oldest.

The gold medal game again pits the U.S. against Canada and it is an odd game for this sort of match-up. Canada scores six runs in the first inning against David Scott and Chuck D'Arcy to go ahead to stay and wins, 11-5. Stofflet relieves in the third and goes the rest of the way. In his 22 1/3 innings, he has given up an unlikely eight earned runs for a 2.51 ERA. Scott and D'Arcy are tagged with the two U.S. losses. The Americans finish the tournament 9-2. Canada has won again.

The preseason is over and the team has arrived in Decatur, IL, for the 1983 national. The Sunners draw the Guanella Brothers again. Ty starts but gives way to Jarvis because of control problems. The sequence of events which result in the relief appearance by Jarvis is important because it says a lot about Ty as a team player.

With the score tied, 2-2, Ty has a rough fifth inning, which includes a walk and a wild pitch. Santilli had been ejected on a disputed call earlier in the game, so Ty asks acting coach Oswald to be taken out of the game (September 12, 1983). "He just felt that he didn't have his good stuff and that Rod, if he had his drop going, would be able to hold them a couple of innings and maybe we could get a run." Jarvis got out of the fifth and sixth innings, but wildness and nervousness resulted in a four-run seventh and the loss.

Jarvis comes back in the second to beat Beer Nuts of Bloomington, IL, 3-1. Chuck Pesce hits a game-winning

Getting Back to Championship Form?

home run. So with a 1-1 record, the Sunners are back in the losers' bracket, and it's Ty's turn on the mound. He faces All-American Bar of St. Paul, MN, which falls, 10-0. The win is Ty's 34th, and puts him third on the all-time list. Only Johnny Spring (44) and Harvey Sterkel (43) are ahead of him.

This game has one of those old time wake-me-ups. The leadoff batter opened with a single that was played into a triple. The next three batters paid for their teammate's show of "bad manners." Rocky was impressed with the three first-inning strikeouts, noting afterward that that was all he needed to see to tell him that this game was well in hand.

The next game, against Page Brake of Salt Lake City, is not classic but it is exciting. Ty is not sharp in the first three innings and goes into the fourth down 3-0. With the bases loaded and down two runs in the bottom of the seventh, Dyke Eck gets a clutch hit that scores two Sunners, moving the game to extra innings. In the ninth, the Sunners load the bases again and this time, Jim Brackin gets the winning hit (4-3). From the third inning on, Ty has not allowed a runner past first as he finishes with 16 strikeouts.

Clear Lake, IA, is next, and Stofflet is the selection. Rocky can be heard reminding his club that they are part of a history that includes a 45-game win streak. Stranger things have happened. This game is classic Ty: no runs, three hits, nine strikeouts. The Sunners get three runs, with Eck again the hitting star. He is now hitting behind Seip, who has shown a tremendous amount of patience throughout the tournament. Each time the Sunners have built a strong inning, Seip is on base.

There is something new about Stofflet that he is not

Softball's Lefty Legend ~ Ty Stofflet

hesitant to discuss. As long as he has command of his pitches, he is willing to be out there in the lead. However, once he notices that he is flattening out, or otherwise losing control, he has no problem making that known to his manager. Also, Rocky is making more suggestions toward off-speed drops that move erratically. Whatever it is, The Sunners are still in the tournament and anything can happen.

The Sunners next meet Pay 'n Pak, the defending 1982 champions. Because of rain delays (and remember this is a losers' bracket game), the game does not begin until 11:30 PM. It ends at 3:30 AM and the old man beats one of the rising stars of the game, Jimmy Moore. Ty gave up a first-inning run and did not allow another until his team was ahead in the 12th, 4-1. It was a 16-strikeout performance, sandwiched around eight hits and six walks. The Sunners had 14 hits while stranding 16.

The most important thing besides the final score (4-3, Sunners) is Ty's jubilation at the end of the game, as he says to H.J. Deitz (September 16, 1983). "I love this game. I love it. I want to let them know I'm here yet, and I'm not too old for this game. Everybody says I'm getting older. I don't want to hear that. I threw like a young kid tonight. Age doesn't mean a thing. On any given day, I can beat anybody."

And so there is a key transition in his thinking circa 1983. "I may not be able to win all the games in which I appear, but if I happen to have my stuff, including my fastball, I'll play anyone, anywhere."

Interestingly, he is giving up everything and nothing with that statement. The cat and mouse game is still being played at all levels. Which Ty Stofflet will be on the mound today, the one who has all his tools or the one who has all

Getting Back to Championship Form?

his smarts? Either way the Tiger has come out to play the game he loves. Are you ready to stand in against him?

Rocky is also jubilant. For the past 14 years, he has rooted for his ace to beat all comers and many more times than not he has come away with victories and trophies that exceed avarice. At some level he can see the beginning of the end, but not tonight. This is the kind of game that makes the hours of preparation seem worth it. When asked about his ace, all he can say is, "He's still the best, no ifs, ands or buts."

Rocky picks Ty to start the next game against Decatur. Unfortunately, he has gone to the well once too often. Ty is strong but not accurate. In less than five innings, he issues five walks and registers no strikeouts. The final score is 5-1 Decatur. The Sunners, once again, have been an exciting team to watch. Their fourth-place finish now qualifies them for next year's ASA National. This is a more optimistic year-end than last and Rocky will, once again, try to figure out how to make the new pieces fit the puzzle.

Stofflet has been rejuvenated by the events of the year, starting with his Clearwater no-hitter and moving straight through to an exciting 5-1 personal tournament record, culminating in an all-night vigil against Seattle's Pay 'n Pak and Jimmy Moore. The game he loves is certainly not ready to let him go just yet.

Taking a Run at Two Titles

THE BANK OF PENNSYLVANIA (BOP) Sunners start the 1984 season with changes in team personnel, as well as changes in the politics of fast pitch softball. As always, some players retire and some move in from other exotic places (e.g., New Jersey and Virginia) to play at softball's highest level. But that part of the game belongs to Rocky. Ty has never interfered with those choices.

The political change in softball is dramatic in that without penalty, teams are now able to play in both ISC- and ASA-sponsored tournaments. This is long overdue but in 1984 is particularly welcome because it will allow the Sunners to appear in the ISC showcase, the World's Championship, to be played in Allentown.

The reader may have noticed by now that the purpose of this book is to follow one man's journey through life. Our initial curiosity has centered on how Ty Stofflet was able to get to the top of his sport while maintaining and preserving an intact sense of self. The title "ferocious gentleman" is meant to capture that duality.

He, better than any of his fellow competitors, was fully cognizant of where he was (inside or outside the lines of play) and of the right codes of conduct on each side of the line. This was true when he began his years in church ball,

Softball's Lefty Legend ~ Ty Stofflet

when he went to the Patriots and Sunners, and later when he completed his career. The man you may have met while he was pursuing team and personal performance goals is the man you will find at some community event today. As they say, "He is very comfortable in his own skin."

There has been a personal evolution in Ty's response to the media ever since the championship years. Whereas he might have been primarily concerned with his performance on the field during the '60s and early '70s, he has accepted his position of prominence throughout the international community of softball as a necessary burden. He is well aware that anything he might say may be widely quoted, but is not at all afraid to point out places where the game itself has become its own worst enemy. In this way he has become an elder statesman rather than a politician.

If you go back to his position regarding Roy Burlison's illegal pitches in the national game that gave his team the win, Ty had many options when asked about his opinion. "The rules are the rules," might have been a politically correct platitude that wouldn't have ruffled any feathers. Instead, he calls the rules misguided and silly for what they are doing to the skill part of his sport. He points out, prophetically, that making the game more technical at a time when interest in the pitching position is at an all-time low is self-defeating.

Ty played within the rules and was rarely called for an illegal pitch, so he is not using his status in the game as a way to improve his winning percentages. Rather, as he explained regarding the Burlison incident, "Roy is a friend of mine." This is no way for the best in the game to be treated. It takes the game out of the hands of its players.

The dual roles of fierce competitor and gentleman

Taking a Run at Two Titles

seem far better suited for the golf course than the softball field. Self-monitoring is not the proper role for any softball player, however when I think of Ty's relationship with softball, it is easy to make a comparison with golf's finest, Jack Nicklaus. Both had an uncanny way of not beating themselves during the most tension-filled moments of a championship. And yet, they were able to appreciate the journey as much as the prize. I have heard both Nicklaus and Stofflet describe a loss as "only a game" – in ways that lesser competitors could never imagine.

Both men could shake off a defeat and go to places to be with their friends. What's the use of being depressed? Everything you had that day was left on the field of play. In the great panorama of life's events, it is unpleasant but acceptable that somebody else gets a chance to be the better player on a given day. For all their greatness, both men lost more championships than they won, and both were known to be gracious in both victory and defeat. In the words of Rudyard Kipling, they were able to "treat those two imposters (winning and losing) just the same."

It takes a lifetime of trials and tribulations to get to that point, but that characteristic is essential to truly becoming a statesman in your sport. By the age of 40, Ty has clearly attained that stature. There are a few times mentioned thus far when others have taken sportsmanship out of the game for the glory of a trophy. In each of those moments, Ty is perplexed, not angry. It's almost as though he is watching a young child who doesn't know any better because he hasn't had the benefit of a solid upbringing. The person is more to be pitied than censured. He can never know the joy of letting his game speak for itself.

Softball's Lefty Legend ~ Ty Stofflet

There is another unpleasant reality that is crowding itself into Stofflet's consciousness. He no longer thinks about games with the invincibility of youth. As each season approaches, he moves farther into softball old age. In 1980, we saw a glimpse of the end of easy wins. For 20 years, good health and a magic rubber arm were accepted facts of the universe, like the day-night cycle or photosynthesis. He didn't necessarily need to know why it happened. He could just be aware that it was a regularly occurring feature of our world.

In 1980 he was in both pain and doubt. Would he ever get back to serious competition? Could he play at a level he would be able to tolerate? Even the City League players who may have resented having to face "the monster" just because he needed the workout, now found that they missed the elegance that he brought to their games once he stepped between the lines of play.

While 1981-83 answered questions regarding his prominence in the sport, his reaction to victories in the nationals sounds more like answered prayers than the supreme confidence that has characterized his prior play. However, this is a story about a man who happens to be a marvelous softball player, not about a marvelous softball player who happens to be a man.

Adaptations and adjustments throughout life are ways in which we keep score of other people's character. Ty Stofflet is a meticulous man who, with the help of a strong family, has kept his priorities in place. He will now have to learn to accept the fact that on any given day he may be the best, or he may be considerably less than best. More than a few players who have stood at the apex of their chosen activity, have been unable to accept a return to mere mortality once nature has moved on to bless the next generation.

Taking a Run at Two Titles

But there is an additional theme that upsets Stofflet's thoughts about his sport. While he is trying to win national and international competitions, the scope of the sport has been losing ground ever since he began playing it. He is clearly playing a game that is woefully behind the popularity of "the anti softball," otherwise known as slow pitch. According to him, they might as well be putting the ball on a tee and calling it tee ball, for all the skill required hitting gravity pitches.

Behemoths swatting slow pitches out of a ballfield does not conjure the elegance of a well executed bunt play or the ability needed to foul off a great drop to keep an at-bat alive. As far as Ty is concerned, politics within his game is seriously interfering with its survival. Anything and everything that can be done to save his sport from extinction should be attempted.

Add to these concerns, the general issues of a father of three girls who are bright, engaging and know how to get their way, and you have what anyone would consider to be a full plate of issues.

At the same time, Santilli has a problem that has been with him since 1971 when he and Ty went to the national and he discovered that the Sunners could play with anybody. Having tasted four solid years at the top, anything less is bitter to the palate.

No matter how he goes about it, Rocky always faces a two-pronged problem. First, how to afford to put a team on the field that can compete in the national, and second, where to find players. Unfortunately, with other teams periodically falling from of the national level of competition, finding good players is less of a problem than finding the dollars.

Rocky finds himself spending far too much time ded-

Softball's Lefty Legend ~ Ty Stofflet

icated to saving his team from insolvency. Kramer to Billard to Hoffman to Reading to BOP may sound like the formula for a spectacular fielding play. Instead they represent the off-the-field heroics of a man who has moved from one sponsor to the next, with all the last minute complications of an episode of the *Perils of Pauline*. There is no doubt that life within the lines was much easier to take than the negotiations that occurred beyond them. All he had to do, once the game began, was to deal with the players and game situations. Relative to his other woes, this was no problem at all.

In a conversation with Bill Miller about Rocky, Bill expressed admiration for the way Rocky handled the behind-the-scenes tasks for his softball teams. "I know that I would never have been able to carry a team without a number of other people helping out. I can't imagine how Rocky put up with it all those years, but he did and he didn't complain."

The 1984 schedule includes trips to Aurora, Decatur, Toronto, and Clearwater, as well as two championship series in Allentown (ISC) and St. Joseph, MO (ASA). Stofflet is again the featured player for this traveling team, but Rocky is going to be careful. While the season is a time for preparation and getting the kinks out, the championships have a feeling all their own. The team's reputation will not rise or fall on the .800 winning percentage it is bound to maintain, but on the number of wins it accumulates when it counts in the national and international record books.

As an aside, when the other players drop off the national traveling tour, they do not necessarily stop playing ball. The Lehigh Valley has plenty of opportunities for the weekday warrior to put on cleats and hoist a few with the

Taking a Run at Two Titles

boys after the game. As his weekly exercise this season, Ty will be playing for Ski Brothers, among others, when he is not wearing Sunners' whites. Joining him will be the "retired" Zeke Delong and Jody Koch. If you're going to play, you might as well put a competitive team out there.

This year Rocky has combined his team with the recently disbanded Linden Merchants from New Jersey. Ronnie Kist, Bobby Lehman, Nelson Walker (p), Harry Griggs and Ricky Popowski, will add to the already talented group that placed fourth in the 1983 national. While this is a good move for the Sunners, it is another example of shrinkage at the top. The Merchants have had a solid record. They have represented New Jersey well in national competition. Their demise is Reading's gain but softball's loss. It speaks too eloquently of the problems that plague the sport.

As the season begins, the Sunners are the class of their competition. They run off a 20-game win streak on their way to the ISC World Fast Pitch Tournament in Allentown, August 10th – 19th. Their first opponent there is Crawford Construction of Savannah. This is Stofflet's first ISC World Tournament game since 1969, when he won for Sal's Lunch. He wins the opener, 2-0, with 13 strikeouts and three hits allowed. They beat a nervous 20-year-old whose wildness allowed the Sunners' runs.

The second game is against the Houston 9 and is well remembered by Jim Brackin, because he takes the blame for the loss. The final score was 4-0, with the Sunners getting only one hit. Stofflet struck out 13 but allowed six hits. If you examine the scorecard, you will find no errors attributed to Brackin, but such was his confidence in his fielding ability that he was well aware that some of the recorded hits could have been called E-6 (error, shortstop).

Softball's Lefty Legend ~ Ty Stofflet

Now Brackin is an ASA Hall of Famer who will twice lead the nationals in hitting. However, this evening against Houston 9 stands out because he let the big guy down in front of the local fans. But here is what Jim remembers after the game. "So I'm sitting there feeling real bad and Ty comes right over to me and says, 'Jim, you've gotten me out of so many jams with your glove. Shake it off, we had a bad game. We'll come back tomorrow and win this thing.'"

Anyone who played with Ty and messed up at a big moment can hear his voice. "You did your best. Put it behind you, and get out there with your head up."

His daughters remember moments when he would walk over to a teammate on the bench who had his head down, speak to him for a few moments and see that person return to the game invigorated. "It's like Dad breathed some spirit back into the player," said his daughter, Brenda. "I don't know how he did it, but it happened quite a lot."

Brackin continues to be grateful for that kindness, 20 years after the event. It wasn't showy and it didn't make the newspapers, but it was something that each of his teammates learned to count on. Jean-Pierre Caravan, who joined the Sunners around this time as a statistician, tells a similar story. "We were in Clearwater to play the Bombers and it was time for the team to go out after the game. Ty looked at me and said, 'You are a full member of this team. Whatever we do, you are welcome to do.'" While he was an honorary captain of this band of brothers, there would be no second-class citizens.

Stofflet goes on to win three games in a row in the losers' bracket. The first is a 7-0 mercy game against Orlando,

Taking a Run at Two Titles

FL. After five innings, a team ahead by seven runs is declared the winner to keep the tournament on schedule. Ty struck out eight and gave up one hit over four innings for the win.

The next two games are both high-scoring affairs with the Sunners beating Pine Grove of Elkton, MD, in the first game and the LOCC Lakers of Portland in the second. Stofflet left the first game ahead, 8-0, but had to return in the sixth to preserve an 8-5 victory. In some ways it is reminiscent of the 28-inning losers' bracket game played for the Allentown Patriots, only this time the pitcher is allowed to sit out the action because of re-entry. In the second game, they beat Portland, 8-3. Seip and Brackin put the game away with home runs.

Reading next takes on All-Car of Green Bay, WI, in one of those Stofflet masterpieces that tend to punctuate his tournament appearances. Reading wins, 6-1, and Ty gives up one hit while striking out 19. While it is a great game for Ty, it lacks the kind of tension that a close game brings to the fans.

Up to this moment in the tournament, Ty has pitched six games in six days. While that is not a particularly awesome feat for a younger man, the 43-year-old knows that he has been through a test. One can hope that the California Kings prove a relatively easy opponent.

Or not! The California game proves to be the talk of the tournament, because it lasts over five hours and takes 17 innings. Keith Groller covered the game for the *Allentown Morning Call* and once again we rely on the reporter's interviews (August. 17, 1984).

The details of the game are as follows: Ty and Peter Finn are locked in a tight ball game with Ty behind, 3-1,

Softball's Lefty Legend ~ Ty Stofflet

due to a Mike Nevin home run. In the bottom of the seventh, the Sunners tie the game on a botched intentional walk to Seip that allowed Moore to score. From this point on, the game reverted to the pitchers' battle that had been advertised. In the ninth inning, a shower stopped play but did not dampen Stofflet or Finn. Their duel lasted until the 17th, when Stofflet allowed a walk, a sacrifice and a couple of wild pitches to bring in the fourth California run. In the bottom of the inning, Seip, Brakin and Clay got hits for the Sunners, who scored twice to win the game.

Ty's interview sounds very much like his reactions after the Seattle game last year. "I still felt pretty good out there," said Stofflet, while mobbed by autograph seekers. "I was just so mad when I threw the wild pitch that allowed them to go ahead."

When asked about his chances of throwing his eighth game in seven days, he says, "I don't know yet. I'll just have to see how I feel when I roll out of bed in the morning. This is just so special for me to do well in front of my hometown fans. I just want to keep them interested and make them happy. They have never seen this caliber of play here before and I want to keep them interested."

Stofflet gets the nod again and goes into extra-innings, 0-0, against Victoria's Jimmy Moore. As has become the pattern, however, magic does not happen twice in a row. In the 11th inning, Eckert hits a home run off a high change-up to win the contest, 1-0. Ray Oswald is left to add his superlatives. "I don't care what anybody says, he's still the greatest in the game. There are a lot of very good kids who can pitch, but Ty is without a doubt still the best. Even at the age of 43."

Ty Stofflet is named the Outstanding Pitcher of the tournament, the first time the award goes to a player whose

Taking a Run at Two Titles

team finishes lower than fourth. Stofflet is the only player on the Sunners chosen for first-team honors. Seip and outfielder Bill Majors are voted to the second team. Decatur, IL, goes home with the championship trophy.

It is fitting that in the year when Stofflet and Brubaker are admitted to the ISC Hall of Fame, Ty goes out and proves that rumors about his demise are exaggerated. The trophy score now includes a 1984 Outstanding Pitcher Award to go along with those of 1967 and 1969.

The Decatur team, that year's winner, has an embarrassment of riches. Bob Ryan has two top-flight hurlers to choose from and he is not interested in selecting an ace. His team has gone through the tournament alternating David Scott (3-0) and Brent Stevenson (4-0). This is the situation that Santilli has sought, to no avail. While Ty's individual feats are amazing, in the big tournaments there is no help in sight.

In September, the Sunners head out to St. Joseph and enjoy a new format. This year's team is seeded fourth and not expected to draw a strong first-round opponent. If you have spent any time in athletics, those are famous last words. Ty starts against San Gabriel, CA, and as reported by H.J. Deitz for the *Reading Eagle*, is called for two illegal pitches in his first three pitches of the game.

However, it is lack of hitting and lackluster fielding that creates a 1-0 loss that haunts the team. "We were in the best bracket we could have been in," Stofflet said. "I can't believe it. I wasn't overpowering, but I still pitched good enough to win." Alan Wishart, the New Zealand native who is pitching for San Gabriel, is mainly impressed that he has a victory over Stofflet. "I've always wanted to play against Ty and any team he is on is a great team. I'm proud to beat a team like that."

1984 - Batting in the local league

1984 ISC World Tourament ~ All World Team

ISC Hall of Fame Player - 1984

Taking a Run at Two Titles

After a victory by Nelson Walker to give the Sunners their first win, Ty is picked to face Peter Meredith of The Farm Tavern of Madison, WI. The game is scheduled for 5:30 PM but with an assist from an earlier, extra-inning losers' bracket game, it finally begins at 1:00 AM. The softball gods shine down on you one day, and make it rain the next.

The final score is 2-1, The Farm Tavern. Ty has been spotted to one run in his two outings. Only one of his three runs allowed was earned, but the team is going home nevertheless.

This has been an unusual year. The excitement of the Allentown tournament has been a refreshing addition to the Sunners' reputation. While they didn't win, they gave the hometown crowd a lot to cheer about. However, in St. Joseph they catch a tournament-seeding break and fall on their face. I am sure that Rocky spent the trip home reminding himself to tell the officials not to do him any favors in future years.

Overall, Stofflet finishes the season 30-8 with an 0.57 ERA. He has provided a new adage. On any given week, he can carry his team to wonderful moments, but now that the DH has taken the bat out of his hands, he can't be the all-tool force when the big games are on the line.

His comments at the ASA national are also respectful of his job as a pitcher at this time of his life. In the past, if the other team scored for any reason, he would put the burden on his shoulders and take full responsibility for the loss. Now that he has learned to live with the skills associated with his new best effort, he can say, "I pitched well enough to win," without it being anything but a factual statement of good effort by a very good pitcher who was not overpowering that day.

Softball's Lefty Legend ~ Ty Stofflet

What I hear with those words is a man who loves the game and is coming to grips with necessary changes that will enable him to stay in the game. About every second or third game he might be overpowering, but he is not willing to wait until those moments present themselves before allowing himself to get out there. Being a pitcher is fun, and he remains among the best of his craft. Adjustments will just have to be a new part of his game.

Gaining Perspective

WHAT WOULD YOU DO if you used to throw a ball well over 90 mph and you were now 44 years old trying to compete among the kids? It is 1985 and the Sunners haven't won a national or international competition in six years. Memories are fading quickly in the manner of something that is receding out of the range of one's rearview mirror. Rocky has moved the team to Allentown in an attempt to capitalize on the excitement of last year's ISC World Championship, but Ty is now an "ageless wonder," coping with the ravages of age just like anybody else.

The Sunners have an excellent team, a tough national schedule, and a mountain of hopes, but there is an unmistakable tiredness that has crept into the rhetoric. If this were some other time in Ty's life, it might make sense to provide specific details of a pre-season's worth of triumphs that would make most players delirious for the accomplishments. For example, there are more no-hitters and the team's 24-game winning streak.

We could also look at Rocky's struggles to stay at the top shelf of the softball wars, but he is once again showing the skills acquired over the past 15 years and keeping his head barely above water.

What I find compelling is the transformation of a per-

Softball's Lefty Legend ~ Ty Stofflet

son of power to a person of almost complete finesse. At the ISC World Championship in Kimberly, WI, Dan Vanderpas of the *Post-Crescent* provides the story and quotes. The headline of the piece is "Ageless Wonder." Dan has watched Ty win a 9-1 game and is in the process of gathering information for his article. "Despite his stature in the sport, Stofflet didn't come off as larger than life, as he chatted the other day at Sunset Point Park. He mingled with the crowd after the team's opening game, sipped a can of beer, signed autographs and jawboned with fans about softball."

The article moves to Ty's family relations. "I never let any of my success give me a big head. My father, who follows me all over creation along with my brother, Larry, wouldn't let it go to my head. If my father saw it going to my head, he would kick me in the behind."

About his pitching, Stofflet admits that he can only reach the low '80s, as opposed to his former top speed. "I have less heat now. I still throw hard at times, but I rely on my changeups and good drops. I'm not a power pitcher anymore. I finesse them more. You go with some off speed pitches and try to make them hit your pitch."

Ty has this to say about studying hitters. "I watch how they stand and where they grip the bat. If they hold their hand down they're going to take good cuts. Then you can fool them. But if they're choked up, you know they're going to punch the ball. Then you got to throw the ball downstairs and inside tight somewhere along the line."

As an American in a game that has become increasingly dominated by Canadians and New Zealanders, Stofflet is asked how he sees these changes. "Softball's a lot tougher than it used to be. The hitters are a lot tougher and the pitchers are coming in from New Zealand and Canada. A

Gaining Perspective

lot of people don't like them coming in, but I think it's helping softball."

Asked about how he wants to be remembered, Ty says, "I want to be remembered as a person who loved to meet people, who enjoyed people. I want to be remembered as a helluva pitcher and a helluva guy."

By this time *The New York Times* has picked up Ty's story and written it as though he remains the fireballer of old, but he will have none of the hype. Playing with these guys means learning to make the best use of the skills he has now. At the time of the tournament his record is 30-4 with 350 strikeouts in 200 innings, but the fear factor is clearly not there.

This is also the first story that mentions family needs and the specter of retirement from the game. It is a piece that conjures up two guys sitting around a ball field, shooting the breeze while one is having a brew. And well it should, because that is exactly what it is.

At the same time, Br'er Rabbit has had a chance to tell the wolf not to throw him in the briar patch because he's old, he's a bit worn out and the thorns would certainly do his sore back little good. In a way, it all goes back to a very old ballplayer fact of life. HITTERS AND PITCHERS NEVER TELL EACH OTHER THE TRUTH. Accurate information can be used against you.

So we have an old young man, or a young old man, struggling to get through the ISC World Tournament. He has learned to speak like a young old man. "I know my limitations," he says, but his on-the-field performance shows little regard for expected human limits (eight championship games in seven days – including two marathons to end the tournament).

When Artur Rubenstein, one of the all-time great concert pianists of the 20th century, was scheduled to play his last concert in Carnegie Hall, he was close to 90 years old.

Softball's Lefty Legend ~ Ty Stofflet

I remember going to the concert expecting the man to cut himself a break and choose a repertoire suited to diminished capacities. He proceeded to tear through some of his favorites as though the infirmities of age could be hung up on the wall and forgotten while he was on stage. I'm not sure what it cost Mr. Rubenstein to push the clock back that afternoon; however it was a tour de force that I will never forget.

In the ISC World Championship, Ty and the Sunners finish fifth. They start off well, with three wins in a row, including Ty's one-hit shutout against Rental Brothers of Saskatoon. A 2-1 Stofflet loss in extra innings to Green Bay puts them in the losers' bracket. Ty throws another shutout against Miller before Dennis Amell, the other Sunners' pitcher, loses to Calgary.

In September, the team goes West to play in the 1985 ASA National Championship in Salt Lake City, UT. Ty will be the ace with Dennis Amell and Rex Giberson chipping in for the Sunners. In the first game, Amell beats Aurora in a laugher, 14-6. The second game against Guanella Brothers seems out of reach as Stofflet allows four runs and is replaced by Amell. Amell has to leave because of a shoulder injury, putting Stofflet back in the game in the seventh inning, behind 4-2. Scott Prescott hits a three-run home run in the bottom of the seventh to give Ty a very unexpected win. This is a good win, but Amell is lost for the rest of the tournament.

In the next game, Pay 'n Pak deflates the legend, scoring an unheard of 10 runs on 10 hits to beat Ty and the Sunners, 10-4. The altitude has clearly taken away something from Ty's ball movement, and Pay 'n Pak is the class of the tournament. Still, he has been roughed up, and Stofflet never took that lightly.

It is All-American Bar of St. Paul that must pay with

Gaining Perspective

the final score, 8-2. Stofflet allows two unearned runs and five hits and registers six strikeouts. Ty's next two games are also wins, over the California Kings, 6-3, and Lancaster, CA, 2-1, in eight innings, on a one-hitter.

The Sunners are assured of fourth place while their ace has steadily moved up the all-time win list to 42, two wins behind Johnny Spring. That, however, is as far as the team gets this year after running into Larry Miller Toyota and losing, 4-1.

Stofflet is 4-2 in this tournament. He garners second-team All-America honors and is two games away from tying his boyhood idol's record for most wins. Br'er Rabbit still has a lot of life in him. His season record is 36-8, but what is most important, he is able to make a noise at the big party.

Wrapping It Up

EARLIER IN THE BOOK, mention was made of Ty's 16 years spent as an active Sunner, with one complete year out for an injury. This is that 16th year. The team is once again based in Allentown, but fan attendance has been a source of disappointment. They are being treated to a sampling of the best softball played in the Western Hemisphere, but their interest seems to have moved on to other things.

Rocky is also facing the same fact that he knew when he generated interest in the championship years of the '70s. It is easier to get people to back a flat out winner, than it is to support an excellent member of the pack. Clearly, it is an exclusive pack, but the Sunners have not been able to rise above third place in any of their six prior seasons. The 1976 game in New Zealand has even gathered some dust.

Team members say the right things. "We are happy to be able to play in the National Sports Festival, etc.," but that's a sort of happiness that does not generate wild partisan enthusiasm.

Stofflet is accepting his senior status with a mixture of feelings. At times he talks easily about the allure of the front porch rocking chair, but if you get a glimpse of his

Softball's Lefty Legend ~ Ty Stofflet

game face, it doesn't fit the image. He has become an "on any given day" pitcher who is not prone to moping about bad defeats or other matters of the moment.

After last year's heretofore unheard of 10-hit, 10-run pounding by Pay 'n Pak in the ASA, he goes out and whips the next three opponents to notch career national tournament wins 40, 41 and 42. The older man is beyond being concerned about a bad day at the office. There is always tomorrow.

Of his teammates, Seip seemed most bothered by the hits that "the unworthy" were able to get during these later years. "There were guys who got so excited about hitting the great Stofflet, when you just knew that they wouldn't have been able to sniff the ball in his prime. I sometimes wondered why he did it."

The phrase "for the love of the game" comes to mind, but knowing Ty, my guess is that every spring offered the opportunity for new experiences to play cat and mouse against the best that Rocky could provide. Ty did not love the game so much that he learned to enjoy being defeated. As long as he believed that he had a real chance to win, that was sufficient to get all the competitive juices flowing.

And this year offers something special that the Sunners are in the best position to provide – a chance to get back to the national and break Johnny Spring's record. Ty is a student of softball history who has always been aware of his place in that history. The all-time wins achievement would be an outstanding addition to his career accomplishments.

If he sounded old at the beginning of last season, this year he sounds young, once again describing a winter-long regimen of bike riding and weight lifting. Of course, it is ironic that his weight lifting days follow his years with Hoffman's York Barbells, but he has found a way to add

Wrapping It Up

strength for the long season ahead, and Ty knows how to work and prepare.

The season will take the team to Seattle for the ASA national, Houston for the Sports Festival, Saskatoon, and Decatur. Clearwater will be coming to Allentown.

In one of his frank, on-the-road interviews in Decatur, reported by Mark Tupper for the *Decatur Herald and Review*, Ty is talking about how it feels to be No. 2 behind Johnny Spring. "If I could win three more national tournament games this year in Seattle, I might just call it quits."

Family is cropping up increasingly among his reasons to move on. "I have three daughters who have played softball. My daughter Kris is pitching right now. I miss being with them. Kris pitched in Philadelphia last weekend and threw a two-hitter with 10 strikeouts. She's doing great. But if she needs help with her changeup or something, where is she going to go? If I'm off in Decatur or some other place, playing ball, she can't come to me for advice. That bothers me."

Ty also expresses an interest in being the No. 3 pitcher on the team rather than the ace. "People expect me to go out there and be great every night and they have a right to expect that. But at my age, I can only pitch that way when I'm fresh. This was my fourth night in a row I have pitched. I felt strong and threw the ball harder tonight than last night. But I missed on some pitches and lost."

Once again Ty expresses his frustration for the piece that Rocky has never seemed to find to complete the 1980s Sunners' puzzle, a top hurler who could allow Ty to step away from the mound, if just to catch his breath. All who have tried out have been talented but inconsistent for one reason or another. With the exception of Bergh, the

Softball's Lefty Legend ~ Ty Stofflet

others have chosen to stay for a bit and move on.

The season preliminaries end and the Sunners set out for the ASA National Championship in Seattle. Earlier, Ty had mentioned that his father and brother have tracked him across the country. That statement is literally true. Harold Stofflet, at the age of 68, has decided to take his 30-foot camper and drive across the country to see his son play ball in Seattle. Driving his rig to see his son is nothing new for the elder Stofflet, but the length of the trip was on Ty's mind. "Boy, I was really nervous until he and my mother arrived in Seattle. The games mattered a lot less. It was good to see both of them arrive safe and sound."

Ty starts the tournament with an extra-inning, 2-0 win. In 10 innings against Plangger's Furniture, he gave up three hits and struck out 13. Later that week, he faced Mankato and also threw a shutout, winning, 5-0, on a seven-strikeout, five-hitter. The Sunners won their next game, 10-3, with Mitch Grey involved in the blowout against the New York Warriors.

After a day's rest, Ty faces Peter Finn and the Midland, MI, Explorers. A win puts him into the record books all by himself, so what does he do, granting the problems of an aging pitcher? He beats Finn, 1-0, on an eight-strikeout, no-hitter. Here is Ty's rendition of the final moment to the local newspaper. "I had a 1-2 count on the batter, and then I called on everything I had ever learned and all the strength in my body. I didn't want to lose that no-hitter – and I struck him out."

Superman has put down his cape and turned into Samson. Fantasy meets reality and reality takes home the prize. For three straight games, the man who needed three wins has thrown three shutouts, including a no-hitter. Remember the comments made much earlier to the effect

Wrapping It Up

that "They can't win if they don't score?" The other teams couldn't because the old guy wouldn't let them.

In the next game, against Pay 'n Pak, Ty battles Jimmy Moore to a 3-3 tie over seven innings. In the eighth, Seattle scores the walkoff run. Ty comments, "Tonight was the night to get him. Jimmy Moore wasn't his best tonight. We had him and we let him off the hook." In their next game, Decatur beats the Sunners, 3-1. Ty lasts an inning and is relieved. All Decatur's runs are unearned.

And so we conclude a definitive chapter in the life of Ty Stofflet. This year he came to establish his place at the top of the winner's standings and with some Herculean effort has claimed the throne. His personal heroics, once again, have earned him All-America status (second team) as he completes a 3-2 record for the year and a 45-16 record as of 1986 in the ASA Nationals.

In later years, he will go on to play for other teams entering the nationals and at the end of 1992, his record will be 46-20, but this is where the individual game coverage ends.

Finishing Up Strong

IN 1987, KIM WAS 21, Brenda was 19 and Kris was 15. Being the father of three attractive, athletic young women was a responsibility that father Stofflet took very seriously. And so, no matter what the attraction of the new year and its softball possibilities, Ty gave up the ghost of leading his team to another national or international championship.

After Reading, there were many ball games in various places, but they had the character of briefly stepping back into the limelight. From time to time, he could prove to himself or the world in general that the combination of his heart, body and brain could create lightning in a bottle just for old time's sake.

Here we go back to the Herb Dudley contests, where the defeat of a 51-year-old Dudley is a watershed event for a team on the rise. As Ty ages, many a younger player gets to live out a dream by, somehow, putting bat on ball. Why does Ty continue to keep a hand in? "As long as it's fun and doesn't stop me from doing other important things, why not?"

The following material was provided by Billy Howell. He was Ty's manager during the period we will be reporting, and he is an ISC Regional Commissioner. According to Billy, a number of ISC World Tournament games in which Stofflet competed between 1989-1993 deserve mention. These are the words he sent me.

"In 1989, I managed Ty for McDermott's All-Star Chevrolet from Baltimore in the ISC World Tournament. In the opening game, Ty pitched against Guanella Brothers, one of that year's favorites to win the tournament. We started the game at 10:00 AM on the upper field in Kimberly, which was quite a hike from the main diamond.

"The game started in front of about 35-40 people. Ty held them hitless for 7 2/3 innings. All throughout the game people keep coming up the hill as word spread about what was going on. By the sixth inning we had a crowd of at least 500 people. McDermott's lost the game, 1-0, in 10 innings and Guanella Brothers went on to take second place that year. Ty was given credit for a no-hitter which occurred two decades after his first one in the ISC world's. After the game, Walt Guanella (the late sponsor) and several of his players came over personally to congratulate Ty on his performance and to breathe a sigh of relief.

"In 1992, Ty pitched with Class Walls of Whiteford, MD. The ISC World Tournament was in Salt Lake City, UT. In his opening game, at the age of 51, Ty pitched a one-hit shutout against Adkins Properties of Houston, TX, winning, 6-0. He lost the second game, 6-0, to Victoria Payless of Victoria, British Columbia. He wins game three coasting to 12-3 final score. Ty wins the next game against Prescott, AZ, 5-2. Ty next wins a complete game, three-hit shutout against Hertz/Capitols of Topeka, KS (3-0). Their last game is against Darren Zack and the Vancouver Magicians. Ty loses in 10 innings, 3-2.

"At the age of 51, Ty goes 4-2 in the ISC World Tournament and wins his final All-World Pitching Honors. This closes the books on his international honors, which began in 1967 and are completed in 1992, representing a span of 26 years."

Of course, there is more pitching to do, and if you happened to see some games after 1992, there is no doubt that you saw whatever he had to offer that day on the field. But all good things, sometime or another, must come to an end, and this is where this part of our story ends.

Finishing Up Strong

Before we reach the epilogue, I have a perspective that I would like to raise, particularly for anyone who has followed the events described on these pages. It is about the title of "best" or "all-time best."

In baseball I would argue that Babe Ruth was a more valuable player, when he was pitching and hitting for his team, than anyone else who ever played the game. This is simply because the Bambino could shut you out and hit one out to beat you. Ty Cobb and whomever else you might mention might have been magnificent at one or more aspects of the game, but not as a pitcher and a hitter in the same game.

Ty Stofflet had a softball career that reads like a fantasy, except that every game detail has been verified by newspaper or official program account. In his trophy case sit the 1976 awards for both Most Valuable Pitcher and Most Valuable Player in the ISF World Tournament. There was no part of the game in which he did not excel, and the tighter it got, the better he seemed to like it. While there may be individuals from other eras who have done things that were his match, the package continues to conjure an exclusive Ruthian comparison.

For what it is worth, I have not heard of anyone who maintained that breadth of extraordinary skills for such an extended period of time. At the age of 62, after health problems, there are still managers who call to see if he can help them capture lightning in a bottle just one more time. And who is to tell them that they can't? Certainly not I.

Ty ~ 1988

Melba, Harold, Kathy & Ty - 1989

Kris Stofflet ~ 1989

Brenda, Kris & Kim - 2001 at Patriots Park

2004 ~ Stofflet children & grandchildren
Top row ~ Kathy, Ty & Andy
Bottom row ~ Spencer, Brooke, Brenda, Kris, Kim & Jake

Siblings Lillian Lerch, Ty & Larry - 2004

Ty & Kathy - 2004

Epilogue

Ty Stofflet in the Lehigh Valley

THIS SECTION IS MEANT TO ANSWER the question, "Is there life after softball for the world class softball player?" The answer is a definite "yes," if the player has had the foresight to design a life that does not center around the erosion of skills or the dreams that might have happened, "if only." Since this book is about a man who possesses a number of skills that enable him to attain his desired outcomes in life, we thought it fitting to complete our story in the present.

Keith Groller has already appeared in the book in connection with the 1984 ISC World Tournament in Allentown, which he covered for the *Allentown Morning Call*. We relied on his articles to provide a flavor of the time, particularly during the California Kings, extra-inning thriller.

Keith was also one of the first people Ty directed me to for some perspective regarding his activities since retiring from active softball pitching. "He's a fair guy, who gets his information right."

My initial thoughts were that Keith would have a lot of background information on Ty the pitcher, but he turned out to be much more interested in addressing Stofflet's contributions to the community. It turns out that the Stofflet legacy is both broad and deep in more places than one would imagine.

Groller began our conversation by noting that three

events occurred nearly simultaneously. "Ty retired, the men's game slipped, and the girls' game gained a strong foothold at Pates Park and at softball fields throughout the region."

"Fathers, who as children and teenagers had grown to love the game of fast pitch by watching Stofflet, encouraged their daughters to play the game. Beginning in the late 1970s and continuing through the 1980s and 1990s, the girls' game flourished in the Allentown area. The same crowds that flocked to watch Stofflet pitch, now swarmed to see 15- and 16-year-old girls do battle under the lights and, in some cases, TV cameras."

Groller noted something quite positive about Stofflet's reaction to the girls' game, as opposed to the kind of jealousy and envy that many other male players displayed toward these upstarts. "He was supportive right from the beginning. Perhaps it was because his daughters, Kim and Kris, sparkled as players. But his relationship with the girls' game extended well beyond his own daughters and Parkland High School."

Groller and Stofflet have spoken a number of times about Ty's love of this sport and interest in supporting the girls' game. Keith recalled, "Ty told me that he didn't have enough time to put into teaching when he had a traveling playing schedule. But at the end of his career there was more time to help his daughters and to help others."

"Because of how much he loved the sport it was natural for him to think about helping the girls become better as the sport was getting bigger and bigger. He also thought that some of the girls could improve to where they could get college scholarships."

Stofflet spoke to Groller about wanting not to rely on his reputation as a way to impress his students. Rather, "He

Ty Stofflet in the Lehigh Valley

became their friend first, and their coach later. Ty told me that the key is for the student to like the teacher. If the kid doesn't like you as a human being, it will be harder for the student to get through to the instructor. If they don't like you, they won't listen to you. Ty's idea is to make his students comfortable immediately. From there everything falls into place.

According to Groller, everything fell into place on June 13, 1996. "It was the day that the Lehigh Valley officially became the Girls' Softball Capital of Pennsylvania and Ty Stofflet's legacy added one more special chapter. It was on that day at Shippensburg University that both the Northern Lehigh Bulldogs and Northampton Konkrete Kids won state championships. Northern Lehigh, located in the small town of Slatington, was the 2A classification champion. Northampton, a much bigger school located due north of both Allentown and Bethlehem, won the 3A crown."

"Stofflet was an assistant coach for Northampton, working closely with their star hurler, Cortney Madea. He had also tutored the Bulldog's star pitcher, Vanessa Strohl, the previous year. He was very proud of their accomplishments that day and told me how hard both had worked, and how hard their teams had worked, too."

Strohl, who went on to star at Kutztown University, finished her senior year with a record of 15-2, a 0.53 ERA and 137 strikeouts in 147 innings.

Madea, who would go on to star at the University of Maryland, finished her final high school season with a mark of 22-1, an 0.86 ERA and 213 strikeouts in 147 innings.

Keith had an opportunity to speak with Medea, and she told him, "Three things stand out when I look back on

Softball's Lefty Legend ~ Ty Stofflet

that season. First, Ty gave me the confidence I never had. Other people thought I was good and I could get the job done, but I never really believed it until I realized that Ty believed in me. The mental game is 90% of the battle. Without thinking and knowing you're the best, you can't be.

"Secondly, without a doubt we would have not won the states without him. He not only gave me the confidence but the rest of the team. Winning is not only about having the best nine players on the field, but rather it's the team that's the best that wins. And that year we defined the term 'team' more than any other group.

"Ty brought us all together. We knew he believed in us, so we believed in ourselves, and didn't for a moment want to let him down, even though he never put any pressure on us. Third, on a personal note, I honestly don't know if I'd be where I am today without Ty helping us out that year. My initial college decision was to attend Lehigh, and then in August, I changed my mind and decided to go to Maryland.

"Part of my decision to go to Maryland was based on a discussion I had with Ty. He told me I needed to get away in order to grow. I didn't know what he meant at the time. I do now." Medea has already earned two degrees at Maryland, an undergraduate and a master's, and is going for her third, a doctorate of law.

Medea also told Groller, "I've realized that the best coaches are the ones that relate the game to life, and see that their players get more from it than how to swing a bat correctly. That's what Ty did in a short season. He instilled confidence in all of us and taught us things that made us what we have become in life."

Medea also remembered one key moment in the 1996

Ty Stofflet in the Lehigh Valley

season, a loss to Northern Lehigh. "After the game Ty came up to me and was shaking his head. He said, 'I'm not going to let this happen to you again. You're not going to lose another game this season.' He was absolutely right. We finished 26-1."

She added, "Ty taught us to play with heart, soul, and determination. Even when we were behind in the bottom of the seventh, we still believed that it was our game because that's the desire Ty instilled in us."

Groller also had conversations with Debbie Anthony, head coach for Northampton, about Ty's influence on the team. "She saw the benefit he brought to the team, particularly during batting practice when he also served as batting instructor. Anthony told me that he would make some key corrections with their hitting. He would also put something extra on the ball when they were going to face a real good pitcher. It gave the girls a big boost to their confidence that they were hitting off Stofflet. He would get a kick out of mixing in his change up for a strike, but some of the girls got better at timing it for hits and that would make him even more happy."

Anthony told Groller, "Ty was never in a bad mood, nor did he ever get angry with the girls and raise his voice like most of us do. He invited the team to his house a couple of times for parties. The girls always knew they could go to him for any reason and he would listen."

One of the things he always did which impressed Anthony was to talk to the opposing pitcher after the game to share some tips or just to congratulate her. He never squandered an opportunity to help someone."

Stofflet told Groller that the most satisfying part of coaching is to see the girls do a good job. "All of the girls I have coached are scattered. It's hard to see them all. But

Softball's Lefty Legend ~ Ty Stofflet

it makes me feel so good when they did what I told them to do and it works out for them. It lifts me up to know that I got through to them and they're producing."

Stofflet believes that there is a danger in girls' psyching themselves out of games. "Before a game, I tell the girls not to think about it too much. I don't want them stressed out. I want them relaxed. I want them to know what kind of pitcher they are, and what they have to do. But I want them to be themselves. I don't want them to do more than they are capable of doing. I don't want them worried about hitters on the other team."

Groller talked to Ty about his earliest experiences pitching. "I remember the first game I ever pitched, I walked 18. But the coach kept me in. He just wanted me to keep throwing. He didn't want me to lose my confidence. If you don't have confidence in yourself, whom would you ever have confidence in?

"You can't go to the mound thinking to yourself, 'Well, I am going to lose. You can't look at the other team before a game and see trouble coming. I don't want my girls to watch the other pitchers warming up and worry about how fast they are. I just want them to worry about doing what they know how to do."

When pitchers come to Stofflet after a bad outing, he first wants to know the direction of the ball. "Was it high, was it low, was it outside, whatever," he told Keith. "I have to ask questions and then I can help them. Hey, everybody has a bad night. I've had more than a few of them. So, when girls come up to me and tell me they have had a bad night, the first thing I say is, 'That game is over and now let's move on.' We start all over again and try to figure out what went wrong."

Ty added, "Again, it goes back to the girls liking you.

Ty Stofflet in the Lehigh Valley

And sometimes, it has to happen right off the bat. Sometimes, you don't get a second shot. If they don't like you they simply won't respond. I know how sensitive they can be. I kid around with them, try to keep them loose and make them laugh, especially after they have made a mistake."

Stofflet tries to make a difference with the parents of the girls he has coached. "So many parents are so hard on their kids and I have had to step in. You try to stop it right away. Some of these parents think their girls shouldn't be making any mistakes. If they were perfect, then why are they bringing them to me? That's why they're here, to learn."

In the end, it is still the allure of the game for Ty and the opportunity to introduce these young people to the game he loves. "I never thought in my time on this earth that I would see what I'm seeing from the girls' game. I can't believe how fast they've come along. Honest to God, I'm amazed how good they have become. I never thought I'd see it.

"They have taken over the game around here. There are so many opportunities for them now. That's why it's worth a shot for them to see how good they can be. We have a great place for them to play in the Lehigh Valley, Pates Park. It's like the Major Leagues for them. I think it has played a big part in the growth of the sport around here."

"But," suggests Groller, "the legend of Ty Stofflet has had plenty to do with it as well. So has Ty Stofflet, the teacher. One of the game's greats continues to make the game great in the Lehigh Valley."

Acknowledgements

AT THE END OF A GAME, it is customary to acknowledge teammates who made contributions to the outcome. This writing game has been thoroughly enjoyable for one simple reason - people found that it was about Ty and went out of their way to help. The outpouring of good will was astonishing to me, both as a person and as a psychologist. If the old saying "What goes around, comes around" has any validity, then Ty Stofflet is a man who has done much good and spread much joy in his life. His friends saw an opportunity to repay him and they were generous.

I am grateful to the Stofflet family, Ty, Kathy, Harold, Melba, Larry, Kim, Brenda and Kris, for making themselves available and being cooperative and candid. Ty and Kathy were consistently hospitable while demonstrating good humor throughout a six-month writing process.

Bill Plummer III, Manager of the National Softball Hall of Fame, was marvelous in his zeal to help us acquire difficult-to-obtain information. He, more than anyone else, seemed to grasp the potential of this project and used his coordinative position in top softball circles extremely effectively. He was also critically important in capturing first-hand accounts of the 1976 ISF World Tournament.

Roy Kortmann, former on-the-field teammate, and current writing partner on other projects, was helpful in many ways in the creation of this manuscript, including gathering background information from softball notables. The final book design and the many changes that preceded it were all influenced by Roy's interest in "getting it right." From the beginning to the end he has consistently provided pleasant, goal-directed support.

Julie Robitaille, owner of Robitaille Administrative Services in Dunellen, NJ, responded rapidly and effectively to tapes created by Roy and myself during the interview phase of this project which significantly moved the process along.

I am pleased to acknowledge six principal sources who provided critical chronological information. Three special people kept detailed scrapbooks between 1970 and 1986: Jerry Heist (1970-1974), Ginny Santilli (1975-1979), and Ed Duffy (1971-1986). Their material was invaluable to my being able to provide specific details of pivotal contests.

The ISC World Tournament information was primarily gathered from three remaining sources: The Allentown Patriots, thanks to Don Hunsicker (1963-1967); The ISC Programs for 1968 and 1970 (courtesy ISC Executive Director, Ken Hackmeister); and ISC Tournament Information (1989-1992), courtesy Billy Howell. Newspaper accounts from the *Reading Eagle* were also independently gathered to illustrate additional regional and national event coverage.

Documentation for the material in this book will be presented to the ASA Hall of Fame. The material was very hard to come by, and those who saved it and made it available for this book have my deepest appreciation.

With Ty and Bill Plummer's assistance, I was able to have extended conversations with a number of former players and officials who performed at the apex of the sport. Each one spent at least an hour speaking on the record about what it was like to play with and against "the ferocious gentleman."

Acknowledgements

Not everybody who was targeted for interviews could be located, but every player or opponent who was found readily agreed to help. Hall of Fame members who were opponents included Tom Wagner, Jimmy Moore, Whitey Parnow and Jim Brackin. We also spoke with teammates, Don Van Deusen, Carl Solarek, Larry Bergh, Zeke Delong, Bob Yoder, Joe Lalli, Jeff Seip, Bob Lehman, Ronnie Kist, Billy Howell, Paul Troika, and Jerry Heist.

Rocky Santilli was particularly gracious in allowing a meeting at his home. His recollections regarding the early days of the Sunners were extremely insightful.

Cooperation from Royce Heath and Floyd Hammen from the ISC enabled us to provide some essential information backfilling in a short period of time. Their support is greatly appreciated.

Allentown Patriot teammate and catcher Phil Schantz was a valuable source of information, as was Jean-Pierre Caravan. I am grateful for their help.

The Clear Vision Publication writer's support team was effective and efficient as usual. You know who you are, and you know how much your support means to me. Thanks for everything.

Last, but certainly not least, my family knows how to be helpful and facilitative at times when deadlines create crises that must be addressed. David's computer skills saved me aggravation more times than I care to consider. The project's aesthetics benefited from Sarah's timely contributions, particularly as in-house photographer. My wife, Patricia, saw the value of this project from its inception and found a multitude of ways to help. She is the rock that allows the rest of us to float freely. Thanks again.

Photo Credits

WE WISH TO THANK the following for permission to use photographs in this book:

- Front cover: Courtesy of the Amateur Softball Association, Oklahoma City, Oklahoma
- Title page: Courtesy of *Allentown Morning Call*, copyright 1988
- Back cover photo of Ty Stofflet, courtesy of the Amateur Softball Association; back cover photo of author and Ty, copyright 2004, Sarah Clarfield.
- Pages 131 & 156 courtesy of the Amateur Softballl Association
- Pages 193 & 212 courtesy of *Allentown Morning Call*
- Pages 30 & 32 copyright International Softball Congress
- Pages 27, 114, 150, 194 & 218 copyright Sarah Clarfield.

All other photographs courtesy of the Stofflet family.